A Study of Bibl...

Just Open
the Door

BIBLE STUDY

(in)courage author
JEN SCHMIDT

LifeWay Press® Nashville, Tennessee

Published by LifeWay Press® • ©2018 DaySpring Cards, Inc.

ISBN 978-1-4627-7988-8
Item 005799554
Dewey decimal classification: 248.6
Subject heading: ENTERTAINING \ JESUS CHRIST--SERVANTHOOD \ STEWARDSHIP

To order additional copies of this resource, write LifeWay Church Resources Customer Service; One LifeWay Plaza; Nashville, TN 37234; FAX order to 615.251.5933; call toll-free 800.458.2772; email orderentry@lifeway.com; order online at www.lifeway.com; or visit the LifeWay Christian Store serving you.

Printed in the United States of America

Adult Ministry Publishing, LifeWay Church Resources, One LifeWay Plaza, Nashville, TN 37234

Author is represented by Alive Literary Agency, 7680 Goddard Street, Suite 200, Colorado Springs, CO 80920, www.aliveliterary.com.

TABLE OF CONTENTS

ABOUT THE AUTHOR..5

INTRODUCTION
Welcome 6
Viewer Guide: Session 1 8

WEEK 1
Why Hospitality?...11
Viewer Guide: Session 2 32

WEEK 2
Jesus as the Model..35
Viewer Guide: Session 3 56

WEEK 3
The Power of One...59
Viewer Guide: Session 4 82

WEEK 4
When Hospitality Is a Challenge...85
Viewer Guide: Session 5 104

WEEK 5
At the Table 107
Viewer Guide: Session 6 128

WEEK 6
The Uncomfortable Yes...131
Viewer Guide: Session 7 150

LEADER GUIDE 152

ENDNOTES 156

ABOUT THE AUTHOR

JEN SCHMIDT

For the last decade, Jen Schmidt has been encouraging, challenging, and cheering on women to embrace both the beauty and bedlam of their everyday lives on her popular lifestyle blog, *Balancing Beauty and Bedlam*.

With a myriad of topics from easy dinner ideas and personal finance to leaving a godly legacy, Jen equips others to live life to its fullest, reminding them it's the little things that really are the big things in life.

A popular speaker, worship leader, and founder/host of the annual Becoming Conference, Jen shares with humor and authenticity as she invites others to join her on this bumpy, beautiful life journey.

She lives in North Carolina with her husband, five children, a few too many animals, and an available sofa for anyone who needs it. For free resources, speaking inquiries, and ideas for all things heart and home, connect with Jen at www.beautyandbedlam.com or @beautyandbedlam.

At (in)courage you are welcome to a place of faith, connection, and friendship, where you will always find yourself among friends. Founded in 2009 by DaySpring, the Christian products subsidiary of Hallmark Cards, Inc., the vision for (in)courage was to create a new home for the hearts of women—where women take turns pulling up a chair to share their stories of what Jesus looks like in their everyday, gloriously ordinary, and often messy lives. Since then, (in)courage has grown into a vibrant community that reaches thousands of women every day, welcoming them just the way they are, offering a space to breathe, loving support, and resources for meaningful connection.

WELCOME!

Welcome, my sweet friend! It's such an honor to have you share these upcoming weeks with me. I'm so excited for all that we're going to learn together that I can hardly stand it. My only regret is that we can't all smoosh around my kitchen table in real life and experience it face to face. I'm typing from that very spot, and my empty seats are begging to be filled by you. I'd keep the coffee brewing strong, while we'd crack open our Bibles together and pore over the truth of what God's Word reveals about the heart of hospitality.

Wouldn't that be wonderful? There's nothing I'd love more than to welcome you into our home and listen to a bit of your story. I'd want to know if you're a mountain or beach, coffee or tea, book or movie kind of friend. Then once we got those simple details out of the way, I'd want to peel back your history, hear firsthand what emotions and perceptions the word *hospitality* evokes in your mind, and catch a glimpse of your precious heart. Unfortunately, all that "in real life" goodness must wait. And it's OK. I can wait, because I know that one day it will happen. It's been promised since the very beginning, and what a day of celebration that will be.

As Christ followers, one day we will feast together in the kingdom of God, encountering hospitality like we could never imagine, but for now, the hospitality we extend and receive on earth is the next best thing.

My goal for the next seven weeks is that you will release your preconceived notions of what hospitality looks like. Throw out your magazines, cast aside apprehensions about your gifting, personality type, or meal-making abilities, and let's look at how the theology of everyday hospitality is intricately woven throughout the entirety of Scripture.

For you, this Bible study may be an invitation to an entirely new way of thinking about hospitality. Or it may be a refresher on what matters most, marked by a new and abiding passion that what you're doing is kingdom work. Either way, you and I will be doing some heart business over these next few weeks, and I pray it revolutionizes your thought process as it did mine.

My prayer is that we'll reframe our picture of hospitality and discover how God uses simple steps of faithfulness to ignite life change. So I'm inviting you to soul-satisfying work that will continue long after these pages are finished.

My goal is to awaken our souls to the transforming power of what open-door living can do in and through the lives of people who step forward and decide, "I'm willing and available." That declaration changes everything.

I want you to be able to look back in one year, five years, and even twenty-five years and glimpse the legacy of hospitality you've lived—the doors you've opened, the chairs you've pulled up to ensure everyone has a seat, the tables extended so that anyone, from anywhere, knows they're welcome at your table. I'm already getting excited, because I know what awaits. You hold the key that unlocks the door to so many meaningful possibilities, and I can't wait to discover them with you. I guarantee it will be worth it.

And I promise, all you have to do is just open the door.

VIEWER GUIDE: SESSION 1

Watch the Session 1 video and discuss with your group the following questions:

1. Take a moment to introduce yourself to the women in the group. Briefly share your thoughts on hospitality. Does it come easily for you, or has it been a struggle in the past?

2. When you read the Greatest Commandment in Matthew 22:36-40, what jumps out at you? Do you find this passage challenging? Or does it affirm that you're on the right track in your walk with Christ? Explain.

3. Do you see the way you love your neighbors as an opportunity to glorify God and show His greatness to others, while depending on His grace to love them well? Why or why not?

4. In her conversation with Jen, Angela Thomas-Pharr relays the story of a woman bringing bread to her home. What "bread" or small acts of kindness and hospitality can you offer those around you?

5. Have you "put life off," as Angela describes it, vowing to offer hospitality after a certain goal has been reached or home improvement has been made? What would need to change for you to be willing to open your heart to hospitality, even if that goal wasn't accomplished?

Video sessions available for purchase at LifeWay.com/JustOpenTheDoor

COME
ON IN

WEEK 1:
WHY HOSPITALITY?

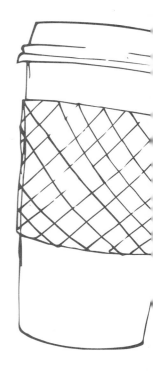

We underestimate the life-changing impact that opening the doors of our hearts and homes to others has on our culture, because we overthink the notion of hospitality.

As I think back on where my legacy of hospitality started, my memories surround our childhood doorway. My favorite days growing up? The ones when the door announced action.

Slam. In. *Slam.* Out.

"In or out?" My mom's voice echoed through the house. "Please stop slamming the door." To me, though, that slam was never one of annoyance. Its recurring sound breathed life. It meant things were happening.

Dropping their mud-covered bikes on our grass, kids stormed through the door, hoping my brothers could play. *Slam.*

A neighbor lady popped her head in, asking for an extra egg. *Slam.*

A missionary family, spending the week with us while home on furlough, returned from an errand or a nearby speaking engagement. *Slam. Slam.*

But more than anything, I remember hearing the sound of that door on Sunday nights.

Long before *Field of Dreams* popularized the phrase, my parents had already personified the message, "If you build it, they will come."[1] Inspired by an outsized vision for impacting their community and a genuine love for others, they defied the indoor space limitations of our 1,500-square-foot house and poured a concrete pad in the backyard. Thus began an informal volleyball league meeting every Sunday night. Friends, kids, and strangers alike gathered from all over. Simple snacks lined the table, complete with stacks of coolers filled with cold drinks. Smoky aromas from a charcoal grill wafted through the air. Laughter mingled with the casual delights of shared conversation, punctuated by roars of cheering and applause for points scored and exceptional plays. High fives all around.

There was never anything fancy about it. But I'm telling you, a whole lot more than volley-ball took place on those incredibly memorable evenings of my childhood. What started out as a loosely-connected community gathering for a game, turned into a group of friends, which lingered into lasting relationships. Life after life. Story after story.

My parents—just an ordinary couple—made a deliberate decision, intent on getting to know the people around them from more than a polite distance. I didn't even realize they were modeling anything special. They were simply living the natural outflow of their faith, putting a smiling face on their hearts of welcome.

It changed the community dynamic. It changed people's lives. It changed my life. Because biblical hospitality has the power to do that. To change lives, to shift the culture, to impact a generation. But most importantly, hospitality offers us a simple yet radical and life-giving vehicle to welcome others and point them to the fullness of life in Christ.

This is a living, breathing, God-ordained path to walk out the abundance of the gospel in our everyday lives through simple acts of hospitality.

Some of you have never seen biblical hospitality modeled well, or you can't conceive why it's so important. You may think it's too late to start now, yet your heart desires to learn more. The exciting news is that your new legacy can begin today. You can begin writing your own open door story right now.

I genuinely believe that lives will be changed with something as simple as an invitation.

DAY 1

The Beginning

"Let's start at the very beginning, it's a very good place to start."[2] I've been humming that musical tune all day, and my mind can't help but leap to the beginning when it comes to understanding the biblical framework for hospitality.

I understand that asking you to set aside years of assumptions on the topic is easier said than done, and I certainly don't want you to forget them; they're part of what shapes your story. The fullness of God's work in our lives is represented by varying personal experiences. When we come to the table with a mingling of backgrounds, nationalities, skin colors, and social, political, and economic differences, it's a vivid reflection of the kingdom of heaven.

Yet after talking with hundreds of women about hospitality, it's clearly a deeply personal and vulnerable act. Our preconceived notions and experiences do shape our views on the topic, which not only impacts how we live it out but also whether we engage and open our doors to others at all.

What preconceived notions and experiences shape your view of hospitality?

Disappointed or discouraged, refused or rejected. Too busy, too burdensome, too much work, too much worrying. Messy house, messy life. Can't cook, can't converse.

Do you find yourself in any of these descriptions? Which ones?

Or maybe you're at the other end of the spectrum: warm and welcoming, inviting, cozy, the more the merrier, open heart, open home.

Over the next seven weeks, we are going to reframe our ideas about hospitality. As we cast a new vision, this will be our opportunity to compare our thoughts from today to what they'll be at the very end of the study.

In school, my least favorite classes were the ones when I'd rush to get there on time, only to have the teacher tell me to take out my pen and paper for a quick quiz. I don't mean to be one of those teachers, but I'm asking you to do the same.

When I hear the word *hospitality,* I think it means:

Please don't write what you think is the correct Bible answer. I'd like you to be honest about this, since no one is going to read over your shoulder unless you want them to.

When I think of inviting others into my home, I feel:

Write down three things you hope your home will be for the people who live there as well as the ones who come over to visit:

As a result of this study, I want my understanding of hospitality to:

In *The Sound of Music*, when Maria taught the children to sing by using the building blocks of Do-Re-Mi, she desired that the children experience the fullness of joy that music would bring them. As they learned the fundamentals, they could compose, create, harmonize, and enjoy a richness they never knew before.

The same rings true for hospitality. As we lay a solid theological foundation and you uncover the depth of hospitality that saturates the pages of Scripture, you won't believe the fullness that accompanies walking a road of welcome. So I officially welcome you to Week 1, not just for our time together, but for laying our first cornerstone. All solid foundations take time, so stick with me because it will be worth it.

The very beginning: Genesis 1:1. You may even know it by memory. How does it all start? Look up the passage, and write Genesis 1:1.

In the very beginning, the Creator, the Sustainer, the Alpha and Omega, offered the first act of hospitality as He welcomed us in His very first week of creation.

After the heavens and earth came into being, each day He continued to create a home for us. With order, beauty, and balance, He hung the moon, the stars, and the sun. He separated the waters from the sky. His detailed designs manifest themselves throughout millions of species of vegetation and living creatures. When He saw it all, He declared it good.

I've read those first verses so many times that sometimes my eyes quickly glance over the intricacies of His creation instead of remembering anew the elaborate masterpiece He created for us to enjoy. They all point to His glory, His power, His majesty, and His goodness.

Rarely a sunset occurs that shouldn't be accompanied by the sky writing, "The heavens declare the glory of God" (Ps. 19:1). His creative expression manifested in perfection.

Yes, God demonstrated His hospitable nature as He welcomed humanity home to live in the beauty of the garden with Him, and then He provided everything they needed.

> The LORD God planted a garden in Eden, in the east, and there he placed the man he had formed. The LORD God caused to grow out of the ground every tree pleasing in appearance and good for food, including the tree of life in the middle of the garden, as well as the tree of the knowledge of good and evil.
> **GENESIS 2:8-9**

Yet knowing what I know now, I'm often stumped as to His choice in Genesis 1:26-27 to make creatures "in his own image." If needed, read Genesis 3 to refresh your memory.

Everything was so good. Why didn't He hang up His paintbrush right before the creation of mankind? He could have finished with perfection, so why continue when He knew what was about to happen? The separation and sin that was about to occur?

Why do you think God created humans, knowing what would happen? Look at Isaiah 43:7 for a hint.

Then with the fullness of His "everlasting love" (Jer. 31:3) for us, God served as the first gracious host as He welcomed humanity to earth for His glory.

When the Holy Spirit opened my eyes to this underlying theme of the hospitality of God, something shifted in my spirit. Having been conditioned to think of hospitality in entertaining terms, the premise that God's perfect character demonstrated ongoing hospitality has revolutionized how I prioritized it.

Think this through. The first invitation began at the beginning of time when God welcomed us to experience perfect life with Him in the garden. It continues to thread through nearly every chapter from Genesis to Revelation. (You'll see this unfold more in later study weeks.) Then it culminates with His final divine act of generous hospitality: the marriage feast.

I yearn for that day when those who trust in Christ will gather at His table in the most glorious act of celebration. Our sin will be no more, and we will sit with God in complete fellowship with Him. (And since it will be the perfect kind of gathering, I'm fairly certain He'll provide chips, queso, and guacamole for me. What will you have?) Yes, God chooses to display His glory, His character, and His everlasting love with sweeping gestures of hospitality, so shouldn't welcoming others be near to our hearts as well?

God's hospitality is dynamic and active. He pursues and welcomes. He rescues and renews. He calls and knocks, but He won't force His hospitality. It's freely given.

From our beginning to our end, He knows our deepest longings and invites us into perfect fellowship with Him, if we will just open the door. He knocks. He first initiates, but then the tables turn, and He becomes a patient guest waiting to be welcomed in.

Read and record Revelation 3:20.

It all points to that invitation, doesn't it? And when you accept that invite, let's get the party started!

DAY TWO

The Heart of God

See! I stand at the door and knock. If anyone hears my voice and opens
the door, I will come in to him and eat with him, and he with me.
REVELATION 3:20

When we brainstormed the title for this book, I'll admit that this verse initially didn't cross
my mind. Perhaps your first assumption gravitated to literal doors, because when you read
the words *hospitality* and *door* on the same book cover, what else would you think?

Any entertaining expert would encourage us to put our best feet forward to make a good
first impression, and that begins with our door, the gateway to our home.

Clear the clutter from the front porch. *Check.*

Hang a beautiful wreath. *Check.*

Arrange the entryway so it's warm and inviting. *Check.*

As we read yesterday about the orderly account of creation, we know God is in the
smallest of details and created beauty for us to enjoy, but His primary focus has always
been on the condition of our hearts.

> Humans do not see what the LORD sees, for humans see what is visible,
> but the LORD sees the heart.
> **1 SAMUEL 16:7b**

As I became more intimately acquainted with the Scripture that explores the heart of
hospitality, I expanded my thought process to include *door* as a metaphor.

"Just open the door" doesn't always mean our personal home. If we're going to understand
the full heart of the gospel, we must begin by asking the Lord to open the doors of our
hearts and soften them to the needs around us. He wants to do this for us. He's opened
my eyes in new ways. He's perked my ears to conversations that I typically stroll by, and
He's revealing powerful stories simply because I'm slowing down enough to open the
door wherever I am.

He's reminded me that every encounter matters to Him, no matter how small it might appear. And let me tell you, when I pray and plead that He'll soften my heart to reveal needs around me, He does it all right—every single time. It's up to me how I'll respond to them.

So when we landed on this title, I sensed Him reminding me of its primary importance through Revelation 3:20. *Jen, this is what it's all about. If they'd just open the door to Me, they'll experience a joy and fullness of life that they never knew existed.* In a surprising role reversal, God, who began as the first host, now awaits the most important invitation of all.

Can a simple invitation really change lives? Oh yes! We open the doors of our hearts and invite Him to be Lord of our lives which then compels us to open the doors of our homes so we can point others to Him. Continuously, we see that modeled in Scripture.

Beginning in the Old Testament, God tells His people to welcome and love the stranger. Within the context of that ancient culture, He instructed them to give of their time, energy, and whatever meager possessions were on hand, demonstrating hospitality to traveling strangers by feeding and housing them after an exhausting journey.

SCRIPTURE PASSAGE	WHO OFFERED HOSPITALITY? TO WHOM?	WHAT DID THEY DO FOR THEIR GUEST?
Genesis 18:1-8		
Genesis 24:31		
Leviticus 23:22		
2 Samuel 17:27-29		
1 Kings 17:10-15		

What theme are you sensing?

How can we practically apply these verses to our lives today?

Did you know that the necessity of hospitality was actually part of their Mosaic Law? Yes, it was the law! Yikes! When I look at how our generation has become increasingly more individualistic and isolated creatures of comfort, I've asked myself, *How much trouble would I have been in back then?*

It was not only the host's expectation to house, offer food, wash their feet, and keep guests from harm; it was an obligation. And these acts were always reciprocal in nature. Considered a breach of honor if either the host or the guest refused, strangers were welcomed as guests and might leave as friends. Communities lived interconnected, and their safety and survival depended on the kindness of strangers.

> *Hospitality in the ancient world focused on the alien or stranger in need. The plight of aliens was desperate. They lacked membership in the community, be it tribe, city-state, or nation. As an alienated person, the traveler often needed immediate food and lodging. Widows, orphans, the poor, or sojourners from other lands lacked the familial or community status that provided a landed inheritance, the means of making a living, and protection. In the ancient world the practice of hospitality meant graciously receiving an alienated person into one's land, home, or community and providing directly for that person's needs.[3]*

The kindness of strangers—it can be a lifeline when we most need it, can't it? One that doesn't need to be reserved for our Old Testament history class or a highlight on the nightly news.

Can you think back on a time when you've been the stranger, the new girl at work, or the uninvited guest who waited on the fringes for a word of welcome? Tell about that experience. Has it impacted how you reach out to others?

Mine was very unconventional, but never have I needed a lifeline so desperately as when I was a college student traveling by myself through Europe. On my way to Bible school with my travel plans derailed, I stood alone in a London train station, wondering where I could lay my head for the next two evenings. Pulling out my list of approved youth hostels, I balanced the dial-up phone (yes, it was a few years ago), my coin purse (back when we needed to insert them every few minutes), and all the adventurous spirit I could muster. Always one to see the glass half full, I made my first call. No answer. *No problem. Lots more options await.* On to the second call. Sorry, no room. *No worries, there are six more to go.*

Painstakingly, I made my way down the list, but call after call ended with no availability. Ten o'clock at night, jet-lagged, travel weary, and a stranger in a foreign land, I flipped to the last listed number as my prior "conquer the world" nerves began crumbling.

An older woman answered. I requested a space, any space, and when she replied that they too were full, I did what any self-respecting girl might do. I begged. I pleaded. I told her I didn't care if I slept on the floor, but I was alone, I had no idea where I was, and I didn't have a place to stay.

"*Please,* can you help me?"

Friend, it was complete and utter desperation.

"We are completely full," the owner replied, "but I guess if you don't mind sharing a bed with Mary, she would be OK with it."

Share a bed with Mary? I didn't know Mary, but I felt an immediate kinship with her, because I'm fairly certain that when Jesus' mother's only choice was to sleep near the animals, she wasn't about to complain.

"Yes, thank you. Thank you," I replied as a strong sense of peace washed over me. Decades later as I recall that story, those emotions still rush to the forefront of my memory, and I'm there in that phone booth once again.

Hailing the nearest taxi, I headed to the given address. As I was greeted by the very proper British proprietor, I lunged into her arms to show my appreciation—so American of me—and my next act still has me chuckling when I think back on this time. I climbed into bed with a complete stranger, better yet, a sleeping stranger. Now granted, sweet, elderly Mary was a retired missionary, and completely safe, or so I'm told, but yes, not only was I welcomed by a stranger, but I slept beside one too.

Recounting this story now, it sounds absolutely crazy. But I think it lines up perfectly with God's plan for offering hospitality to strangers in need, and I guarantee, I was in need.

All these years later, I can't picture the face of the woman who showed me such kindness, but I'm still grateful for her gift of an invitation when I needed it most. It felt radical to this overwhelmed traveler who desperately yearned for someone to offer grace and a simple welcome.

> Have you had a similar experience of welcome? Tell about how you were made to feel at home.

This experience marked me in such a profound way that my heart for the stranger, the lonely girl, the one waiting on the outskirts to be invited in, has impacted my heart for gathering.

There's a reason God impressed the importance of showing love to strangers throughout the Old Testament. We see it found in Leviticus 19 when God commanded Moses to tell the Israelites the following:

> When an alien resides with you in your land, you must not oppress him. You will regard the alien who resides with you as the native-born among you. You are to love him as yourself, for you were aliens in the land of Egypt; I am the LORD your God.
> **LEVITICUS 19:33-34**

> Write these verses in your own words.

The Israelites were intimately acquainted with what it felt like to be strangers, foreigners, and hostages of their hosts. Once chained by the bondage of Egypt, they understood freedom and God's merciful rescue. And when they didn't have a home, God provided food and shelter as the Hebrew people wandered in the wilderness (Ex. 16–17).

God wanted the Israelites to remember their own desperate loneliness, their struggles, and their years in slavery, so they could empathize and create a safe space for others who needed to be welcomed. There was another reason that God called them to care for the foreigner. They were to model for all the surrounding nations what a relationship with God looked like and who God is. They were to show that God wanted to and would welcome the foreigner into a relationship with Him.

> For the people of God in the Old Testament the duty of hospitality came right from the center of who God was. I am the Lord your God who made a home for you and brought you there with all my might and all my soul. Therefore, you shall love the stranger as yourself. You shall be holy as I am holy (Leviticus 19:1). Your values shall mirror my values.[4]

That's the cornerstone of why hospitality matters so much. It matters to the heart of God. It is foundational to His nature and to our theology of hospitality. This heart of the gospel that's rooted in a gift of invitation weaves its way throughout all of Scripture, and we've only touched the surface. When we welcome and invite others into community, it's because we're driven by an overarching principle: love God, love His will, and point others to His glory.

Since we've started at the very beginning, let's remember why we are here. Prior to our salvation, we too were strangers, foreigners, orphans to God, and separated because of our sin. Yet because of His hospitality extended to each of us, we are strangers no more. Jesus opened the door for us to have an everlasting, personal relationship with God.

> So then you are no longer foreigners and strangers, but fellow citizens with the saints, and members of God's household, built on the foundation of the apostles and prophets, with Christ Jesus himself as the cornerstone. In him the whole building, being put together, grows into a holy temple in the Lord. In him you are also being built together for God's dwelling in the Spirit.
> **EPHESIANS 2:19-22**

> Take a moment to close in prayer, thanking God for His love and for welcoming you into His household. Ask for His guidance to extend the same to others.

DAY 3

Biblical Hospitality

I admit I throw the word *love* around much too liberally. As I write, I'm sitting with my candle burning, a fuzzy blanket covering my lap, and soft music playing in the background. I love it. The best part is my hot coffee in hand. I love my morning coffee. I also love French fries dipped in ranch dressing. I love a good book and a movie. I love watching our children enjoy spending time with each other. So many things I love. For me, it's birthed from my passion and zeal for life, but I don't want to become numb to the fullness and depth of its true, biblical meaning.

Nothing compares to the love that Jesus spoke about when challenged by one of the Pharisees,

> "Teacher, which command in the law is the greatest?" He said to him,
> "Love the Lord your God with all your heart, with all your soul, and with
> all your mind. This is the greatest and most important command. The
> second is like it: Love your neighbor as yourself. All the Law and the
> Prophets depend on these two commands."
> MATTHEW 22:36-40

The word *love* used in these verses stems from the Greek *agape*. *Agape* is defined as "to esteem, love, indicating a direction of the will and finding one's joy in something or someone."[5]

What stands out to you about this definition of *love*?

With the fullness of the meaning fleshed out, let's look at the Greatest Commandment again. Everything good that His Spirit produces in our lives comes from a single-minded devotion to these two priorities: love God and love others. When we resolve to embrace an open-door lifestyle, the one word behind this motivation is simple too—love.

Love is our invitation to act, and our choices launch from this cornerstone. Note that Jesus didn't pause and ponder part two of His command. He didn't divide these two instructions into an either/or situation.

The way we love our neighbor reveals something about the way we love God. And the way we love God reveals something about the way we love our neighbor.

> I have loved you with an everlasting love;
> I have drawn you with unfailing kindness.
> **JEREMIAH 31:3, NIV**

We are to pour into others with that kind of love and kindness. I want my love for God and His love for me to spill out to those around me in such a tangible way that they can't help but wonder what makes me different.

Don't you want the same? Don't you want to be known as someone who lives Life with a capital L, fully alive in Him and loving others so thoroughly because you have no doubt from where that *agape* love stems?

Does that reflect you now? Why or why not?

Can you think of someone who lives fully alive like that? Share about her.

I refreshed our memories with the Greatest Commandment, because somewhere along the way we've made loving others more difficult than intended. We've forgotten that opening our hearts and homes to others, and loving our neighbors as ourselves, has nothing to do with our entertaining skills; it's all about showcasing the love, grace, and mercy of our Lord.

Look up 1 John 4:19, and write out exactly why it is that we love.

Paul reminded us that it's about sharing our lives.

Because we loved you so much, we were delighted to share with you not only the gospel of God but our lives as well.
1 THESSALONIANS 2:8, NIV

One of the easiest ways to show love is to invite others into community with us: to practice hospitality.

In the New Testament, we find the difference between a friendly and generous reception (the dictionary definition) and what we are called to practice in biblical hospitality.

Read Romans 15:7. What is a primary motive found here for hospitality?

Different translations offer varying verbs in this verse: "welcome" (ESV), "receive" (KJV), "accept" (CSB), but each of these end with for "the glory of God."

The Greek root expands on *agape's* meaning even further:

> To take to oneself, i.e., use (food), lead (aside), admit (to friendship or hospitality): to take or receive into one's home, with the collateral idea of kindness.[6]

This is our motive for living a life of welcome, yet sometimes we allow social entertaining to hijack the heart of biblical hospitality. When I'm stressed and overthink why I invite, I'm reminded that we have no grand blueprint for hospitality aside from loving others. As the master architect, God drew up hospitality so that it's anchored to this core component— loving Him and loving others.

Among the most direct, concise biblical statements on this subject is what Paul says in Romans.

Pursue hospitality.
ROMANS 12:13b

It's not a question. In fact, *pursue* is a strong verb that implies constant or continuous action, a proactive decision. When you break down the word *hospitality* from the original Greek word *philoxenia,* it's a combination of two concepts. *Philos* is one of several words

for "loving," while *xenos* means "a stranger."[7] The concept behind hospitality has its origin, literally, in love for outsiders.

> Don't neglect to show hospitality, for by doing this some have welcomed angels as guests without knowing it.
> HEBREWS 13:2

Yet somehow, there's a misnomer that these verses only apply to those who have the "gift of hospitality." Many assume it's an optional, bonus suggestion for those who love having people in their homes and throwing parties, but nowhere in Scripture does it suggest that some have the gift of hospitality while others lack it. Instead, we're repeatedly told in Scripture that the Lord chooses to receive and multiply the smallest offerings we have to give.

He didn't first clarify the challenge to welcome with a list of expectations. Nowhere can I find in the Bible, "Pursue hospitality, but not until you've mastered ten tips for hosting a beautifully organized dinner party." We aren't given any qualifications about our personality types, the size of our homes, or the ingredients necessary for a culinary delight.

There's such freedom in that, isn't there?

While some may like creating lovely tablescapes more than others, that has nothing to do with the heart of hospitality. Every single one of us is meant to be in the habit of pursuing hospitality—opening our doors to love those around us. Grammar gurus will notice that it's an imperative sentence: a command. Yes, it's both a calling and a command to love others well in a tangible way by continually pursuing hospitality.

To further clarify, let's look at the differences between entertaining and biblical hospitality.

In her book *Entertaining,* Martha Stewart says,

> *Entertaining, like cooking, is a little selfish, because it really involves pleasing yourself, with a guest list that will coalesce into your ideal of harmony, with a menu orchestrated to your home and taste and budget, with decorations subject to your own eye. Given these considerations, it has to be pleasureful.*[8]

This one paragraph hints at the telltale difference between the two. It all rests on this dichotomy.

The entertaining host seeks to elevate herself for personal approval. And as Martha mentions, it's a bit selfish. When the guest arrives, the entertainer internally announces, *Here I am. Come into my beautiful abode and have the honor of partaking of all the wonderful things I've spent hours getting done for you. Look at this lavish buffet, the intricate décor, and the wonderful party favors. How fortunate for you to be here and be part of this.*

While I embellish on what a hostess might actually say, we've all encountered this once or twice, haven't we? Maybe we've even allowed a similar tone to slip ever so subtly into our own hosting.

Friend, I can tell you right now, this will be one of the greatest areas of tensions experienced as we make opening our door a regular rhythm of everyday life. Why should this surprise us? Once again, it stems from the very beginning with Eve's temptation in the garden to want more, to be more impressive—it stems from our pride.

Satan is crafty. Why should he switch up his strategy now when it's worked so well since the first place people called home?

However, biblical hospitality is different. It's not about us. Opening our doors has nothing to do with the actual setting, the guest list, or the food. The atmosphere can be exactly the same with very different results based on the heart attitude of the one who welcomes.

While we may use our love of beauty and creativity to pamper our guests if we choose, the goal is to reflect the heart of God. Welcoming others as He Himself has welcomed us.

So where do we start? The verses below give us an idea of the character qualities that enable biblical hospitality.

> Look up the following and write down how we are to welcome and treat others.
> Romans 12:10
>
>
> Ephesians 4:1-2
>
>
> Colossians 3:12-13

Read Philippians 2:3-5. How do these verses tell us to act? Who is the model or standard for our actions?

Biblical hospitality offers our best to Him first, understanding that our best to others will then fall into place. It transforms our selfish motives and elevates our guests. When the hospitable hostess swings wide the door, all her attention focuses outward while expressing, *There you are. I've been waiting for you. There's no one more important today than you, and I'm thrilled you're here.* The posture we assume in hospitality is one that bends low, generously offering our hearts to another despite whatever interruption to our own plans or comfort. Extending hospitality is about freely giving of ourselves while granting others the freedom to be themselves. Shifting our focus from us to them removes all unnecessary expectations. No need to worry about what to say or how to act. Just come as you are because our approval is only for Him.

Hospitality, unlike entertaining, treats everyone as guests of honor rather than grasping at honor for ourselves. It is servanthood, not status-seeking—"there you are," versus "here I am"—serving others instead of serving self.

The deep-seated worrying, the excuses, and the overthinking of a simple invitation should be warning signs, telling us we're confusing social entertaining with hospitality.

When we realign ourselves with the ultimate purpose of hospitality, the blessing comes in the difference. For as we obey what God commands here—as we begin to experience the fullness, richness, and joy that comes from practicing life-giving hospitality—we see this biblical instruction transforming from an active command to a deep, profound, yet simple calling, one that we pursue first out of love, only to find it too contagious for us to stop.

When we use our lives exactly as they are, desiring only to create a sacred space for our guests, mixing it with the countercultural truth of loving Jesus and loving others, we turn entertaining upside-down, and it becomes radical hospitality.

To know Him and make Him known. All for His glory.

HOSPITALITY INVITATION

Generating a legacy of welcome begins with one small step of faithfulness at a time, so each week, I will invite you to join me in a simple challenge.

I've often dubbed myself as the "Queen of Best Intentions," meaning I want to be intentional with my choices, but I don't always follow through. These challenges are meant as an encouragement to close the loop on best intentions and make them a reality.

We've already looked at the Greatest Commandment: loving God and loving our neighbor as ourselves. But today we are going to rethink it in terms of proximity, in terms of our actual, literal neighbors. Begin with the ones who live next door, those people with whom we're too embarrassed to initiate conversation because we can't remember their names. Or how about the couple who recently moved in across the street, the ones we've avoided ever since our trash can rolled into their yard and they got upset about the mess? Maybe it's the neighbor who shares the apartment wall, whose loud noise brings constant annoyance.

Simple steps can change the way we do community with those who live in closest proximity to us. Little decisions can reveal the great needs waiting out there, crying to be met, as we open our literal doors. To befriend. To be a light in the darkness.

What does it mean to really love our neighbors? Not with an agenda. Not as a project to check off our to-do lists. This is about cultivating an authentic relationship with people we live (and work) closest to and then letting God do whatever He desires to do with it from there.

My fear is that we've sort of generalized this concept of neighbor, to the point where we miss the specificity of the command and don't even apply it to those people who are our most obvious neighbors, the ones we most often see in passing. That's why I'm issuing a call to begin putting this principle into practice right where we live, work, or volunteer.

As I think through how to love them well, I first imagine ways in which I want to be loved. Encouraging words or simple acts of service are always great beginnings to any neighboring relationship.

PLUS ONE

This week it's about adding a "Plus One." No, we're not looking for a future husband or a date for a wedding, but we will seek to add one new conversation, one new act of kindness, or one new opportunity to connect in a more meaningful way with someone outside our normal interactions.

Let's ask ourselves a few questions as a starting place. Remember to turn your grace on and your guilt off. We are starting our new legacy of hospitality today, and I can't wait to see how your answers change over the next few weeks.

Think of the eight closest apartments, homes, or work cubicles/offices. Jot down the names, occupations, or any personal information you know about the lives of those who live or work there.

1.

2.

3.

4.

5.

6.

7.

8.

How did you do?

Statistically, more than half of us don't even know our neighbors' names, let alone have a relationship with them. And even among those who do know their neighbors a little, who talk to them once in a while, nearly all of them (when asked) say they've never had any meaningful interaction with a neighbor. It's almost nonexistent. As Christ followers, we must do better.

> This week, pick one person from your Plus One list to initiate some kind of new conversation, interaction, or if you're ready, invitation.

To get the ideas going, how about starting with the neighbor whose name slips your mind? This week make it your priority to watch for a time to connect with her. Take the first step and bridge the disconnect. If it's been months since you've talked, humble yourself, and say something like, "I'm so sorry that I haven't taken the time to get to know you more. I want to change that. I'm so embarrassed, but please remind me of your name again. I'm Jen." Leading with honesty and vulnerability serves as a bridge builder. If you have extra burgers on the grill and see them in the yard, sometimes a spontaneous invitation works wonderfully and eliminates prior pressure to go crazy cleaning.

Do you pass someone in your work cafeteria every day but have never asked them a personal question? Maybe today is your day. I'm not suggesting any kind of church-related conversation either. I'm encouraging a "Hey, I'm so glad it's Friday, aren't you? Do you have any fun plans?" Casual. It starts there.

> From your Plus One list, identify one thing you could do every day, by word or action, that builds the relationship with no ulterior motives except glorifying God through one simple relationship builder.

Remember, Plus One. I can't wait for you to see what happens when you incorporate one small step of intentionality.

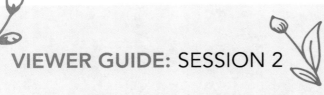

VIEWER GUIDE: SESSION 2

Watch the Session 2 video and discuss with your group the following questions:

1. How might you "cultivate a spirit of welcome" in your home with guests, friends, and family?

2. Jen said, "Whenever you apologize for your messy house or your chaos, it still makes it about you. Stop apologizing because it doesn't point others to Him; it points to yourself." Have you ever thought about that before? Do you agree or disagree? Why?

3. How was hospitality modeled for you in your home of origin? What from that experience do you hope to emulate in your home as an adult? What might you like to do differently?

4. What does the statement "our legacy starts today" mean to you? Does it bring you comfort or anxiety? Why?

5. In your life, what might it look like to, as Donna said, "Live on purpose in telling the truth"?

6. Do you rely on other people to extend hospitality to you before you reach out to them? Do you struggle to "go first" in relationships? Why might that be a temptation?

7. Jen says, "Adoption is the heartbeat of the gospel." How might you be a part of God's plan of adoption in the world? Consider ways to help through adoption of children, discipleship (helping usher people into God's family), or supporting foster and adoptive families.

Video sessions available for purchase
at LifeWay.com/JustOpenTheDoor

LET'S GET COFFEE

(OR TEA)

WEEK 2:
JESUS AS
THE MODEL

More than twenty years ago, our move from Wisconsin to North Carolina didn't come as a surprise. We prayed about it, planned for it, and sought wisdom from trusted mentors on whether we should plant new roots so far away, but nothing had prepared me for the loneliness I would experience those first few months.

We said goodbye to family, our jobs, our church home, a lifetime of shared memories, and many deeply-rooted relationships. I knew we'd been called to make this move to North Carolina, but—exhausted, homesick, and isolated—I still struggled with starting all over. New situations are hard, but I wasn't prepared for how difficult this transition would be.

I did know that if I stayed hunkered down with our two small children, I'd slip deeper into isolation. I challenged myself to step outside my comfort zone, so I packed up my diaper bag and visited a local moms' group.

It took three visits, but one woman sought me out and invited me to a playdate at the park. I counted down the days, and when it finally arrived, she ushered me to a picnic table topped with a cheery floral tablecloth that she'd scattered with simple "grown-up" snacks for us to share. While the kids played, she breathed life into this soul-weary mama.

I was stunned, surprised, grateful, and overwhelmed by this simple act of kindness.

At a time when I ached to be included, God knew I craved a reminder of His constant compassion. Through my new friend's extended invitation, she modeled Jesus' kindness and pursuit of me, a gracious example of how I desired to welcome others.

Through her life-giving hospitality, she "put on love" (Col. 3:14) and became the hands and feet of Jesus in a very practical and tangible way.

As a sidenote, the phrase "put on love" in Colossians 3:14 has no actual verb since it is used in the imperative tense. Instead, it pulls the verb phrase "put on" from verse 12. So when verse 14 says to "put on love," it's a command, not merely a suggestion or a nice thing to do. As believers, we are commanded, "Beyond all these things *put on* love, which is the perfect bond of unity" (NASB).

My new friend also reflected Ephesians 5:

> Therefore, be imitators of God, as dearly loved children, and walk in love, as Christ also loved us and gave himself for us, a sacrificial and fragrant offering to God.
> **EPHESIANS 5:1-2**

Can you imagine if each of us stepped forward as His image bearers, believing that our gift of an invitation would be that lifeline for someone else this week, month, and year? Can our pursuit of others shift our culture at work, church, in our neighborhood, or anywhere we travel? Can drawing someone else into a connected community change lives?

I believe it can. I know it can. I've witnessed it, and you will too.

DAY 1

He Pursues

Our house sits in the middle of some fairly dense woods. With five children, it's offered up a haven for every kind of fort-building activities you can imagine over the years. One afternoon our son called to me, "Mom, we can't find Emma. She was just here."

Not alarmed, I assured him that she was only hiding from her brothers, but then one minute led to two and two to ten, and in the span of those brief six hundred seconds, my heart expanded with love, desperation, and heartache in ways I didn't know possible. You see, there's a creek that runs beyond our property, and while she'd never wandered that far before, my mind immediately went to the possibility of what might happen if I didn't bring her home before she reached that point. I never knew my legs could run so fast. With dogged determination, I pursued, chased, shouted, cried, examined every inch of our woods, and threw in a bit of full-blown panic for good measure. We finally found her. She was hiding. As a game, she'd chosen to conceal herself amidst the thick foliage and refused to answer us when we called. This mama was not a happy camper, but when I found her, when her precious face met mine, her sin, her foolish choice did not matter one bit to me in the moment. And while there were later consequences in hopes she would not consider that again, the relief I experienced and my love for her only knew one thing: my mama's heart would have done anything necessary to find her and bring her home.

Have you ever had a similar experience? What emotions ran through you?

As I uncover the depths of God's hospitable nature—the enormity of how He loves us, protects us, pursues us, welcomes us, and seeks us out—it's nearly impossible to fathom. My desperate longing to find our daughter was only a small microcosm in comparison to His pursuit and desire to belong with us. Even though our sins are many, His love, grace, and mercy are so much more than we can imagine.

This morning I meditated on Psalm 139. I've read it many times, but today I read it aloud with fresh eyes.

Read aloud verses 1-17. Don't be shy. There's such power in the spoken Word. Pay special attention to the active verbs and what they describe. Highlight them or write them in the margin. There's nothing like declaring God's truth out loud.

Because the Word is alive and active, it speaks something new each day. Jot down key phrases that breathed life to you today.

In verses 1-6, we discover God's omniscience.

> The word omniscient, *which has been part of English since at least the beginning of the 17th century, brings together two Latin roots: the prefix* omni-, *meaning "all," and the verb* scire, *meaning "to know."*[1]

As I personally reflect on His omniscience, I can't help but respond in gratitude.

Oh Lord, I am so unworthy of the way You search for me. You know every hidden crevice of my heart and understand me more than anyone. Before my journey even began, You went into my future to prepare a way for my past. It's such a breathtaking reminder that not one single detail of my life doesn't pass through Your hands of presence first. My joys, my sorrows, my dreams, my struggles—nothing surprises You. Thank You, thank You. There's such a glorious intimacy in how You know me like no other.

Sweet friend, no matter how you feel today, whether filled with doubt or grief, insecurity or fear, God is near to you and desires fellowship with you. Do you believe that?

In verses 7-12, we witness God's omnipresence: He is all present. It's impossible to flee from God. When we feel lost and unseen, He loves us so desperately that He will storm the gates of heaven and never stop looking until He finds us.

There were seasons of my life when these verses didn't hold the comfort they do now.

Have there been times when you've struggled to be at peace with God and felt the need to escape?

What drew you back to Him?

Sometimes in our unconfessed sin and doubt, it's our natural instinct to flee and hide from Him. We are that child in the forest hiding under the thick foliage, but there's nowhere we can escape His great love for us. When we feel far, God is near and will drop everything to find us. Regardless of your choices, He adores you so much that He still seeks you out.

There is nothing we need to do first. He doesn't need us to accomplish His divine purpose, yet even before He created us, He chose to do life with us. He loved us with an everlasting love and set about to woo us and call us nearer to His heart (Jer. 31:3). To realize that we are the object of His affection stirs in me an elevated understanding of our two-fold mission of loving Him and loving others.

Christ's abundance in our lives is astonishing, and it all happens at God's invitation. Don't you want to be on the receiving end of Christ's love? Better yet, don't you want also to introduce others to His same generous offer? When our faith is focused on the Great Inviter, we live in response to who He is in our lives, and then our love is a natural overflow of His presence. We no longer have to serve others or pursue hospitality because He commands it. Rather it becomes a blessing that we get to extend: a grand opportunity to be part of His divine plan in making God known.

What task do you often think about with a "have to do" attitude?

How might it help to start thinking about it as a task you "get to do"?

Let this new perspective soak deep into your bones. What a privilege. When your heart and mind focus on His great love for you, then you're able to fully understand the joy of offering life-giving hospitality.

Recently, a woman commented to me, "Jen, I've watched the way you pursue people. You seek out the ones who aren't included, and I appreciate that about you." I shared with her a bit about my Hospitality Manifesto:

> *May our home be a safe, refreshing haven where everyone is loved, valued, and welcome—a soft place to land where real life happens. When guests arrive, may they sense a joyful, "Welcome Home" spirit that points them to Christ, and may it permeate in such a way that every single person feels as if they can truly make themselves at home. Our home is a place where everyone is welcome, yet may I never wait until I'm ready to swing those doors wide open, because if I wait, it will never happen.*

Modeled on Christ's pursuit and inclusion of us, its foundation not only encourages me to practice hospitality, but also reminds me to include daily rhythms of kindness, generosity, and presence at home and everywhere on the go.

My desire is to exude Christ's joy and initiate gestures of kindness. The day-in, day-out challenge to pursue holiness can get easily swept aside amidst my own agenda. Rush, rush, rush. *What do I need to do? What can I cross off my to-do list?* If I'm not intentional about incorporating a daily rhythm of welcome, my choices revolve around me, and I miss meaningful opportunities to open the door to others. I incorporate a written reminder (or a phone alert) that challenges me to be intentional with my day-to-day activities. When I see the reminder, I ask the Holy Spirit to reveal unseen needs that I otherwise rush by. *Lord, show me one person I can love on today. Who needs a word of encouragement?*

What my friend didn't realize was that my pursuit of others also stems from being intimately acquainted with the pain and loneliness of being on the outskirts looking in, wanting to be welcomed and invited, yet not quite there.

As women, our hearts ache to be included. Knit into our DNA is a hidden longing for deeply-rooted relationships that journey through life with us: someone to notice, acknowledge, and see us right where we are with no ulterior agenda. And while no one can know us fully or fill our intimate longing in the way that God can, He has designed us to come together in community because He created us for fellowship. We aren't meant to do life alone, yet we often find ourselves in that very spot. Because of His great love for us, we now have a choice to create community or continue in complacency, to seek others or sit alone, to welcome or worry, to invite or ignore.

Circle which of these you tend to do more naturally:

Create community	Continue in complacency
Seek others	Sit alone
Welcome	Worry
Invite	Ignore

What are some small steps you can take to begin to live more in the left column of that list?

For me, the pain of being uninvited birthed an intentional calling to look for the lonely, unseen girl hiding in the corner, the woman on the sidelines, or the one sitting at a table by herself. I think of the intensity in which I searched for my lost daughter and what it would mean to a lonely woman if I could offer a fraction of that love to her.

I'm not implying that it's easy to implement or that there aren't a host of potential obstacles standing in the way, but the choice should be obvious. We step forward in love because how we love others says a lot about how we love God. How we pursue community reflects the heart of the gospel.

In Luke 15, Jesus tells three stories to drive home one, overarching message. As you read these verses, note that regardless of why something (someone) is lost, Jesus' relentless pursuit of us never changes.

All the tax collectors and sinners were approaching to listen to him. And the Pharisees and scribes were complaining, "This man welcomes sinners and eats with them." So he told them this parable: "What man among you, who has a hundred sheep and loses one of them, does not leave the ninety-nine in the open field and go after the lost one until he finds it? When he has found it, he joyfully puts it on his shoulders, and coming home, he calls his friends and neighbors together, saying to them, 'Rejoice with me, because I have found my lost sheep!' I tell you, in the same way, there will be more joy in heaven over one sinner who repents than over ninety-nine righteous people who don't need repentance."
LUKE 15:1-7

How diligently did the shepherd pursue the lost sheep?

What was his reaction when the sheep was found?

I love this imagery from *The Expositor's Bible's* retelling of this parable:

> *Suppose you have a hundred sheep, and one of them, getting separated from the rest, goes astray, what do you do? Dismissing it from your thought, do you leave it to its fate, the certain slaughter that awaits it from the wild beasts? or do you seek to minimize your loss, working it out by the rule of proportion as you ask, "What is one to ninety-nine?" then writing off the lost one, not as a unit, but as a common fraction? No; such a supposition is incredible and impossible. You would go in search of the lost directly. Turning your back upon the ninety and nine, and turning your thoughts from them too, you would leave them in their mountain pasture, as you sought the lost one. Calling it by its name, you would climb the terraced hills, and awake the echoes of the wadies, until the flinty heart of the mountain had felt the sympathy of your sorrow, repeating with you the lost wanderer's name. And when at last you found it you would not chide or punish it; you would not even force it to retrace its steps across the weary distance, but taking compassion on its weakness, you would lift it upon your shoulders and bear it rejoicing home. Then forgetful of your own weariness, fatigue and anxiety swallowed up in the new-found joy, you would go round to your neighbours, to break the good news to them, and so all would rejoice together.[2]*

Now look at verses 8-10:

> Or what woman who has ten silver coins, if she loses one coin, does not light a lamp, sweep the house, and search carefully until she finds it? When she finds it, she calls her friends and neighbors together, saying, "Rejoice with me, because I have found the silver coin I lost!" I tell you, in the same way, there is joy in the presence of God's angels over one sinner who repents.
> LUKE 15:8-10

What was the woman's reaction when her money was finally in her hand?

Since we are called to "be imitators of God" (Eph. 5:1), what do these passages mean for you personally?

How could this impact your understanding and practice of hospitality?

All those feelings, the searching and seeking, the pursuing and prioritizing, the welcoming and celebrating regardless of the circumstances, the vast scope of love that we study in those passages, I want to apply to my understanding of hospitality. Our heavenly Father never stops pursuing, so why should we?

DAY 2

Hospitality on the Go:
Walk the Road of Welcome

My Norman Rockwell image of cozy, home-based hospitality was dropkicked into the end zone when I first realized that Jesus, the One we model hospitality after, never had a permanent address.

If I peeked at one hundred of our study guides from last week's definition of *hospitality,* ninety-nine of us likely mentioned something having to do with hosting people in our homes, right? Yet our Lord who embodied the ultimate lifestyle of hospitality—the style guide, the living portrait of all things welcome—never owned a house, but He still initiated hospitality everywhere He went.

Throughout Scripture, this amazing Host teaches what it means to invite others into a new way of life, yet He never stayed in one place for long. He always traveled where needed, and met people where they were at in the most unlikely places, creating a safe place of belonging as He walked.

> Read 1 John 2:6. From what you know of Jesus, how did He walk?

Jesus walked the road of welcome and offered the gift of invitation whenever, wherever, and with whomever He came into contact. He is still the embodiment of all things Home.

> How does that revelation transform how you think of engaging others in your day-to-day life?

> How do you take your cue from Jesus by taking your hospitality on the road?

If your schedule looks anything like mine, this could be an aha moment like it was for me. While Scripture is clear about its mandate to welcome others into our homes, this gives such freedom to proactively choose an enlarged vision of hospitality that looks different from what we originally imagined. The essence of hospitality stems from our spiritual hearts, not our physical homes.

Paul reminds us that, "Because we loved you so much, we were delighted to share with you not only the gospel of God but our lives as well" (1 Thess. 2:8, NIV). I can share my life. Anything I know about gathering people I learned from Him anyhow, so if Jesus walked the road of welcome, so can I.

This doesn't mean it comes easy. I remember stewing with resentment for weeks after our kids signed up for football. Our schedule was already crazy and then we added practices that I'd unknowingly agreed to. Personal time was nonexistent and the "real" ministry opportunities I wanted to be a part of fell by the wayside.

One day, it was as though the Lord tackled me (it was football after all), saying something like, "Jen, quit complaining and wasting time. You signed up for this and agreed to this schedule, so choose to bring Me glory in the midst of it." That's when my aha moment hit. I couldn't quite contain my newfound excitement. When I thought I didn't have time to add one more thing to my plate, I saw how the Greatest Commandment, Christ's Great Commission, and sharing my life with others could intertwine on the sidelines.

I laced up my shoes and got walking right to the sidelines of our kids' sports field. I embraced my new motto, "Hospitality Will Travel" and added it to my manifesto, and it completely shifted how I did life with others. I looked at how Jesus modeled His Father's love in tangible ways as He walked the road of welcome by extending simple, intentional invitations. Often, He connected meeting a physical need with a spiritual need.

Look up the following verses and fill in the chart below.

VERSE	JESUS' INVITATION
Matthew 4:19	
Matthew 11:28	
John 1:39	
John 7:37	
John 21:12	

We learn to make room for one more because He first made room for one more. We invite others to the table because He demonstrated the beauty of life done together. We initiate, invite, and gather because He did it first. He is the model of all things welcome and His invitations are simple.

> Oh, how we love to complicate this! How have you overcomplicated the thought of living a life of welcome like Jesus modeled for us?

With footballs flying around me, I made a conscious choice right then and there to alter my attitude. I released my previous plans for those free practice hours and instead of viewing them as something I had to endure, I offered them to the Lord and reminded myself, *Jen, you don't have to; you get to.*

For the next few months, the sidelines became my new home, and the families involved became my people. I packed up my love of hospitality and brought it with me to the football field, while the Lord and I exchanged a few high fives over the idea that this is where He'd placed me for this season. Different nationalities, different social and economic backgrounds, varying political affiliations—He'd brought them all to this field and put them right in front of me. "Look what you *get* to do," I could almost hear Him saying, "go have fun!"

That year was revolutionary. I approached practice time with an elevated vision. I'd sit on the bleachers, on the sidelines, or behind the concession stands, wondering those earlier questions, *Who can I love on today? Who needs encouragement?* Nothing fancy. No special skills needed. No agenda. I started paying attention. I started observing. (If I'd had a phone at that time, it would have meant turning it off and looking around.) I brought blankets, snacks, and toys for our babies and asked other moms to join me. The blanket became our table and the two-hour practice a bridge for new community. Even on those days when this mama arrived worn and weary, I had no special expectation except, *I'm here to share life with you. Come sit if you want.*

> Look up Matthew 28:19-20.

We've all probably heard plenty of sermons on the Great Commission. It can seem daunting, overwhelming, and even scary. We might feel guilty because we don't have

the time or resources to fly overseas and take the gospel to the ends of the earth. We may wonder if we're capable of clearly articulating the good news so that we do the gospel justice, yet in this context, it all changes.

Go, as translated here, means "journey" or "walk" or "travel."[3] I think we can raise our hands high, feeling like we are always going somewhere (maybe too much). So pack up your pursuit of hospitality and offer it to others as you walk through your day-to-day activities.

On those football sidelines, as I looked to my right and left, God had brought the nations to me. Women sitting beside me needed the love of Jesus, and I knew how to share it because I needed it myself. And let me tell you, He started showing up in that place, right there over the kids' Goldfish® crackers and applesauce.

It's a pretty radical concept. Hospitality as an on-the-go lifestyle. Hospitality: will travel. But since when has anything Jesus modeled turned out to be anything less than radical?

> Make a list of ways you can take your hospitality on the go. Where do your feet take you every day? How can you walk the road of welcome today? Be as specific as possible.

It may mean opening your car door to offer a friend a ride or opening your office door during a lunch break to share a few minutes of conversation—anywhere God has planted you for a season, or even for a thirty-minute lag between other appointments.

Remember my new friend who invited me to a simple picnic in the park? I've thought through why this impacted me so much. She anticipated my need. She initiated a basic invitation of welcome. She took her hospitality on the go. She fed me, but understood that extravagance wasn't necessary—her simple gesture spoke love in volumes.

Friend, this is something we can all do. A tablecloth, a few snacks, no emphasis on perfection, yet her small acts of kindness lavished His abundance on a restless soul.

Please don't underestimate this. Living on mission is a powerful force. God has called, equipped, and appointed you to do amazing things right where you are—in whatever role you work or serve. Look for those opportunities. Pay attention and seize those moments. At school, at the grocery store, with neighbors, or wherever, you have the opportunity to be the difference in someone's seemingly ordinary day.

> So here's what I want you to do, God helping you: Take your everyday, ordinary life—your sleeping, eating, going-to-work, and walking-around life—and place it before God as an offering. Embracing what God does for you is the best thing you can do for him.
> **ROMANS 12:1, MSG**

It's hard to say no to hospitality on the go when God's asking you to offer whatever is already on your schedule to Him.

As I type this, our football player is getting ready to play his final collegiate game. It's been fourteen years since I first offered my makeshift blanket table to others. If you'd have told me then that the launching pad for our family's greatest area of spiritual significance would occur by pitching ourselves on the sidelines of a sports field and taking our hospitality on the go, I'd have stated, "That's not possible." I would have been wrong.

The power of your faithful presence, showing up over and over right where you're planted, can change a generation as you welcome others and point them to the Ultimate Inviter.

I can't wait to hear what your extended invitation is going to be.

DAY 3

Hospitality as Worship

We passed in the hallway and I spontaneously offered, "Let's get coffee sometime." A few weeks later, she sat in my family room clutching her coffee cup like a life preserver.

"No one knows all that's happening with me. I took a leave of absence from work due to severe panic attacks, and I haven't left my house in weeks. Even when I woke up this morning, my heart battled at the thought of coming to your house since I don't really know you. I needed and wanted to come, but I was paralyzed. My mind kept telling me not to go."

Inside of an hour, our relationship had quickly moved from "Hi, how are you?" acquaintance status to sisters, with hearts woven into a kinship known only through a shared story of struggle.

"But it's the first time I've felt a sense of joy and anticipation in a long time," she went on as tears streamed down her face. "I need community and I want friends, but I've been so afraid to put myself out there because sometimes the rejection isn't worth it. When you followed through on your invitation for coffee, I started crying."

I sat stunned. How had I so misjudged her? She seemed to have everything together.

Mentally, the problem fixer in me started trying to figure out ways to comfort her when this was so outside my realm. *What words could I say?* More than that, I kept thinking, *Why me? Why had she entrusted her heart with me? And how could I begin to steward her trust in a way that honored the Lord and my new friend?* I was at a loss.

> I'm sure you've been in a similar situation when a friend poured out her heart to you. How did you respond? If you haven't been in this situation, how do you think you would respond?

> Write out Galatians 6:2.

How does this verse tell us we can serve one another?

How does this relate to the Greatest Commandment?

The Greek root for *bear* in Galatians 6:2 means "to lift, literally or figuratively (endure, declare, sustain, receive, etc.):—bear, carry, take up."[4] The Greek root for *burden* in this verse means "weight."[5]

Who do you see carrying a heavy weight or load around in their own personal lives?

How can you help lift some of their weight? Bear their burden? Fulfill the law through love?

In that moment, I knew the best I had to offer her was to simply be present. Sometimes that's enough. In fact, sometimes it's the perfect response, the best of all other options. Sometimes the people before us just need us to be silent and sit with them in their deepest time of need and help bear their burden.

This is not always easy. I wanted to give a quick solution, but her deep ache couldn't be fixed through my trite words. What she felt could only be fully remedied by the master Healer.

So I sat. I listened. I grabbed her hand and looked her in the eyes. I slid over a tissue box. I refilled her coffee mug and listened some more. Every once in a while, she'd ask for my words, but I kept them few. All she really needed was the ministry of my presence. She needed listening ears, a tender heart to receive her, and the knowledge that in those moments nothing was more important to me than being fully engaged in our time together.

I approached her with my own apprehension, choosing my words carefully.

"I don't know where to start, because I feel any of my words will sound trite. One thing I know to be true is that you are loved, and there is no one who understands your grief, your panic, or your suffering more than Christ. I can tell you, too, that I am here for you. And with you. And for as long as you'd like to stay, you are welcome. We have all afternoon."

And that's what we did over the next few hours. We stepped forward toward the One who modeled compassion. I canceled my afternoon plans and our coffee date extended to a simple salad lunch. Somewhere between chopping the broccoli, dicing the chicken, and mixing the salad, my bone-weary journey joined hers. We cried together. We prayed together. We shared our story of God's goodness amidst our difficulty, and we pointed to the One who redeems these moments. We were both deeply moved.

I still don't know how it happened—how a simple coffee invitation between two relative strangers opened the door to this authentic mingling of spirits: a sacred space created where boundaries were destroyed and defenses diffused. I only know, through the ministry of presence, the Holy Spirit swept in, opened our hearts, took hold of any preconceived agenda, and gave us a glimpse into how the early church in Acts practiced hospitality. I understood it even more intimately now, why it was so central to the biblical narrative. I sensed God's presence in the practice of it, where both host and guest received blessings of abundance.

That afternoon marked another significant perspective shift in how I viewed living a life of welcome. It was the purest form of hospitality I'd experienced: a holy time, an act of worship, where our hours together were aimed at the glory of God.

It's where I began to see my offering of hospitality as a sacrificial act of worship.

What do you immediately think of when you hear the word worship?

Read Romans 12:1 again, this time from the Christian Standard Bible:

> Therefore, brothers and sisters, in view of the mercies of God, I urge you to present your bodies as a living sacrifice, holy and pleasing to God; this is your true worship.
> **ROMANS 12:1**

I want you to note the last phrase in varying versions: "your true and proper worship" (NIV), "your reasonable service" (KJV), and "your spiritual service of worship" (NASB).

Did you notice that the words for *worship* and *service* in these translations are interchangeable? It led me to explore other areas where this might be the case. As I dug into the Hebrew and Greek roots for *worship,* my heart recalibrated how I approached this gift of welcome that we have the opportunity to extend. The words *worship, work,* and *serve* are used interchangeably in many verses throughout Scripture.

> But as for me and my house, we will *serve* [work, worship] the LORD.
> **JOSHUA 24:15**

> This is what the LORD says: Let my people go, so that they may worship [serve] me.
> **EXODUS 8:1**

For me, this changes everything. Not only do we understand hospitality as a spiritual act of service but also as worship.

The biblical essentials of worship flow directly from God's Word. As the psalmist declared,

> Ascribe to the LORD the glory due his name;
> worship the LORD
> in the splendor of his holiness.
> **PSALM 29:2**

Those declarations aren't confined to a church service or Bible study. There's such freedom in realizing that as our hearts bend low before the Lord, any chosen gospel-focused act that elevates His magnificence, any heartfelt, Spirit-led response that brings Him pleasure, encompasses worship.

If the basis and aim of all biblical worship is the glory of God, then when we choose to welcome others into our lives with this goal, that response of hospitality is worship.

> Hebrews 13:15-16 combines two New Testament forms of worship.
> What are they?

What might be the outcome of only using words in our worship?

Authentic worship means honoring God with more than just our words.

In 2 Corinthians 8:5, we're reminded we are to give of ourselves "first to the Lord and then to [others] by God's will." Our worship, our service, our love for others communicates a lot about what we believe about the character of God—and that knowledge gets me passionate about living more intentionally.

Does this idea of "hospitality as worship" shift your view on welcoming others? How so?

It's shattered my image of needing perfect lives and perfect spaces. When I witnessed how a cup of coffee offered to a distant acquaintance could overflow into worship and healing, I realized biblical hospitality is much more than our latest dinner party.

Hospitality is a deep and mighty investment, not just for those around us, but it's an investment in our own souls.

Remember, don't overthink it. There is no right or wrong to-do list that needs to be generated. Through worship, we must act and we must respond, but *that* we respond is so much more important than *how* we respond.

That's the beauty of perfectly imperfect hospitality. It's fully leaning into the truth that it isn't about us. As contrary as it feels, since we're doing the inviting and hosting and possible cooking, it's simply not about us. But it does involve us and desperately needs our surrender for it all to be about Him.

When we walk this road of welcome, I can make no guarantees of its outcome, but I do know that over and over He takes our meager offering, multiplies it, and shows off His goodness for all who are ready to receive. What a unique privilege hospitality gives us to share this deep heart need for community, spread some of the joy we've received as a result of knowing Him, and in the process, worship the One who is worthy of all our praise.

HOSPITALITY INVITATION

It's hard to find a reasonable excuse for saying no to traveling hospitality when it doesn't even interfere with your busy schedule—because you're already there!

For me, it took chiseling the chip off my shoulder, handing my crazy schedule over to God, and inviting others to join me on my blanket—my new home away from home, my open door out on the open road.

Earlier this week, I asked you to list places that you could bring your traveling hospitality, but now I want to take that general suggestion to real life implementation.

> Grab your calendar, planner, or phone—whatever you use to keep track of your schedule—and observe where you'll be in the coming days. Who will be along your road?

> Pick one person each day to whom you can bring a word of welcome, a lunch invitation, a handwritten note, or even something as simple as a slightly more personal conversation.

When I did this a few months ago, there were flowers at the grocery checkout lane marked down. I bought three bundles and asked the Lord to show me who needed extra encouragement that day. I handed them out with a "Just because I'm thinking about you" word of blessing. Two of the three recipients texted me later sharing details that I could never have known about their difficult week. Small acts of kindness and hospitality matter.

> Right now, set a reminder in your phone or write it in your calendar.

VIEWER GUIDE: SESSION 3

Watch the Session 3 video and discuss with your group the following questions:

1. Have you struggled with seasons of apathy in your walk with God? Describe how God helped you walk out of that apathy. If you're in a season of apathy now, how might you walk out of it?

2. Jen says, "Jesus gave a gift of invitation wherever He went." How might you follow His model in initiating and pursuing those around you?

3. Take some time to brainstorm ways you can practice hospitality on the go by offering generosity, words of welcome, and kindness in everyday moments.

4. Do you see your daily tasks as ministry (vocation, parenthood, marriage, etc.)? Why or why not? Do you strive to glorify God in your work and in your home? Name ways you're doing this well and a way in which you want to improve.

5. In conversations with those around you, do you use listening as an open door to care for others?

6. How are you intentionally leaving a legacy of hospitality in the world around you? If this is a new idea for you, how might you start implementing some ideas?

7. Jen said, "Our calendar speaks to the priorities in our lives." How are you aligning God's priorities with the time in your daytimers? Does something need to change?

Video sessions available for purchase at LifeWay.com/JustOpenTheDoor

HOW ARE YOU?
(REALLY)

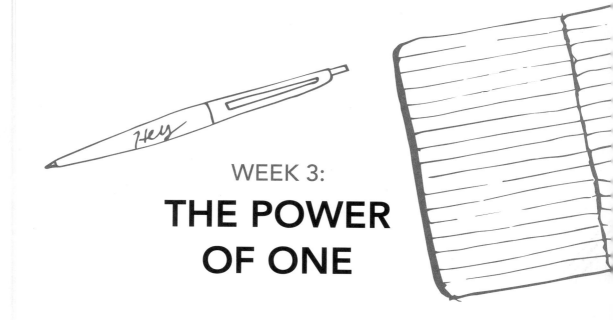

WEEK 3:
THE POWER OF ONE

In the middle of the frozen food aisle, I "did" church. Right in between the tater tots and frozen peas, I almost missed it, and I'm so grateful I didn't.

I observed the oddest pairing of shoppers: an elderly Caucasian man and a young African American man pushing a cart together. Admittedly, I started eavesdropping on their conversation.

The boy held up two items and he contemplated, "If I buy this, it's twice as much as that, so I can't afford both." He put the treat back, and the man gave a short commentary about his budgeting decision.

I can't begin to explain how this moment impacted me. I'd stumbled upon an older man mentoring a younger man on the simple tasks of grocery shopping. A daily act that many of us take for granted.

I wanted to yell over the loudspeaker, "Life-changing legacy on aisle seven. Pay close attention. This is how we do life together."

No one else seemed to notice.

There's no time to second-guess when the Lord directs you to speak encouragement, so I approached them with my sister-in-law.

"We didn't mean to eavesdrop, but we wanted you to know how special it is to watch your relationship. I wished we would have had someone teach us how to shop."

For a split-second, I panicked. *How will they respond? Did we offend? I better clarify.*

"It seemed like you were shopping together. We love seeing you do that as a team."

For the next forty-five minutes, we did church together in an inner city grocery store as Kaqueen, a 20-year-old African American man, attempting to find focus for his future, and John, a 77-year-old Caucasian man, shared their unique story of friendship and struggle.

"I told him he should consider the Army as a possibility," John informed us. "Why should he struggle and work three jobs to make ends meet? We live in a tough place to change our lives, so I'm letting him live in my apartment until he can get on his feet. I want more for him. I don't have any children."

Kaqueen added, "But I'm his number one son. I love hanging out with him more than my own friends. I learn things that I would never think about with my own friends."

We looked him in the eyes and said, "The world needs young people like you who are being mentored and anchored, because then you can share your story and make a difference for others. We believe you are going to be a world changer."

In a matter-of-fact manner, Kaqueen replied, "I don't exactly know what that means, but I think I believe that."

I told him, "Twenty years from now, you'll be shopping with your own children telling them what an impact John had on your life. This is a beautiful picture of what the world needs. Life on life, black and white, young and old, inter-generational friendships encouraging one another."

"Yeah, we should be on TV," Kaqueen determined.

"Yes," we chuckled in agreement. "This would make the best feel-good Hallmark® movie, because it's all true."

This week, let's dive into the life-changing impact of life-on-life hospitality. There are Kaqueens and Johns waiting to share their story, and you never know where the Lord will ask you to share yours.

DAY 1

The Multiplication Process

I'm not much of a math girl. Never have been. In fact, I fight the urge now and then to count on my fingers. (Phew, I've never admitted that before, and I feel so much better now.) Give me all the books and words, and deep, lingering conversations, and you'll have me for a lifetime. I know my day would be better if you were sitting next to me, snuggled up on our porch, sharing life together over a hot cup of coffee or iced tea—pick your beverage of choice. So although I never mastered Algebra, the Lord had a sense of humor when my religion professor executed a math problem, which both stunned me and revolutionized how I invested my time in ministry.

That one moment in time marked such hope for me.

Young, bright-eyed, and eager to brainstorm ways to make our worldwide mark for Jesus, my classmates and I touted grand ideas and lofty opinions on best practices and benefits of large-scale church programs versus small groups, and after a few minutes, our professor stopped us.

He demonstrated the multiplication process that would occur if each one of us purposefully invested in the life of one other person that year and then continued with a new person the following year, and so forth. He issued us a challenge: form one friendship in which we'd unpack the teachings of the Bible together, study sound theology, and unfold how it interacts and impacts all aspects of our lives. Then encourage our new friend to do the same with another person the following year.

Then came the kicker. He asked us to estimate how many lives this ripple effect would personally impact if each of us took his challenge seriously over the course of a lifetime.

Would you care to take a guess? Come on, give it a go.

I told you math is not my strong suit, but imagine if we each made this one-life-a-year investment. Multiplying ourselves starts out slow, so after the first year, there would only be two disciples, and by the end of the second year, only four women would have been reached. By the fourth year, sixteen, but here's where the numbers snowball. By year twenty five, together our multiplied efforts could reach millions of people. A verse from Job began to take on new meaning:

> Though your beginning was insignificant,
> Yet your end will increase greatly.
> **JOB 8:7, NASB**

While I'd like to think that a basic multiplication problem ushered in my newfound sense of hope and purpose, I know that ultimately the Holy Spirit was using that simple tool to peel back layers of my insecurity and ignite my heart in new ways. I knew two things. I loved Jesus, and I wanted others to grasp the power of His love and the fullness of joy that comes from knowing Him as well, but I didn't know the next steps to take. I felt this sense of urgency, but I felt woefully unprepared (or so I thought). I wasn't qualified in any notable ways, and I assumed becoming a woman of influence required a carefully-sketched, bullet-point plan with knowledgeable insights to memorize and a carefully-curated PowerPoint® that culminated in a grandiose gesture, leaving others riveted and wanting more of Jesus, who I knew and loved.

Remember, it was college. High achievers, dreamers, and doers—who encouraged me to think bigger and bolder, not smaller and certainly not solo—surrounded me.

While my personality tends to be a visionary with an approach to life that dares to dream, I can't tell you the number of times I've overthought a situation and then never took action. As I glanced at that board again and took in its meaning, something transformational occurred. The weight of others' unrealistic expectations for me crashed to the ground. I experienced absolute freedom. I wanted to jump up on top of my desk with pom-poms and a megaphone—I had much more energy then—and yell, *I don't have to do it all, but I can do that one thing now! Yes, I can! Invite one person. Please Lord, show me what to do next.*

> Have you had a moment like that—when the Lord ushered in a new truth, you felt a new freedom, and you were excited to share it?

Even after twenty-five years, I'm still overwhelmed with gratitude that God uses the most unlikely followers to bring Him glory and impact His kingdom. Sometimes I'm amazed He uses me in spite of myself.

When Jesus bypasses the seemingly powerful leaders and teachers in the Bible, and goes the extra mile to seek out the unqualified, everyday, average men and women to minister His gospel in extraordinary ways, He assures us that our smallest offerings amidst His grand plan do matter.

Our beginnings may be small, but they are significant (Zech. 4:10).

We are going to spend some time today getting to know a few women of significance. Some of their stories you've likely read many times before, but once again, we're reminded the Word is alive and active.

> For the word of God is living and effective and sharper than any double-edged sword, penetrating as far as the separation of soul and spirit, joints and marrow. It is able to judge the thoughts and intentions of the heart.
> **HEBREWS 4:12**

Ask God to give you a fresh perspective. Remember, He wants to do that for you.

As you read, envision what it would have been like had you lived during this time. Read the surrounding context and put yourself in each woman's shoes. What were some of the struggles they faced? How did God use their everyday activities to bring Him glory? I've filled in the first one for you.

ORDINARY WOMEN GOD USED FOR SIGNIFICANT THINGS			
WOMAN	SCRIPTURE	CHARACTER QUALITIES	HOW SHE RESPONDED TO GOD'S CALL
Mary	Luke 1:26-38; 2:38	Found favor with God	Obedience and praise
Mary of Bethany	John 12:1-11		
Mary Magdalene	John 20:1-18		
Tabitha/Dorcas	Acts 9:36-43		
Lois and Eunice	2 Timothy 1:5		

What do these women teach you about God's ministry model?

God's "way is perfect" (Ps. 18:30), and He chooses to use ordinary people to do kingdom work.

Why do you think God chooses to work this way?

I think back on that college religion class and how the Lord stopped me in my tracks that day. It was as if He said, *Jen, My story is going to be written in your everyday moments. Start today by opening your door.*

There are only a handful of times when I can pinpoint the Lord impressing on my heart something so clearly, and while I wasn't quite sure what He meant at the time, I took Him literally and opened my door, my dorm room door to be exact. I called the local Youth for Christ ministry office and sought out a high school girl struggling with some dark influences in her life. I welcomed her in, offered up my hand-me-down sofa, a listening ear, continuous prayer, and I pointed her to the Source of our only living hope, because honestly, I had no clue where else to start.

I took my cue from Paul's refreshing vulnerability in 1 Corinthians 2:1-2 and admitted it. And you know what? She didn't mind one bit.

> When I came to you, brothers and sisters, announcing the mystery of God to you, I did not come with brilliance of speech or wisdom. I decided to know nothing among you except Jesus Christ and him crucified.
> **1 CORINTHIANS 2:1-2**

Then I took Him at His Word again and made 1 Corinthians 10:31 a part of my ministry model.

> So, whether you eat or drink, or whatever you do, do everything for the glory of God.
> **1 CORINTHIANS 10:31**

What would such a ministry look like in your life?

Is there anything ordinary when we do everything to the glory of God? Absolutely not, so I started with Rice Krispies Treats® and Diet Dr. Pepper® and offered up our time together for His glory.

Right then in my messy dorm room, I once again experienced biblical hospitality as an act of worship. It didn't take a big budget or delightfully decorated dinner parties. He didn't ask this go-with-the-flow extrovert to get her organizational act together.

He starts by asking us to open the door to just one person and point them to a life of abundance in Him.

As I think back on key milestones in my own life, every single one is marked by an invest-ment from one woman committed to sharing life with me for a season. Their impact wasn't a result of a larger-than-life platform or words crafted for their blog. No, women who believed in the beauty of being deeply rooted right where God had placed them changed my life through everyday encounters. They weren't looking to be launched into a more impressive opportunity. They had nothing to gain from their time with me; yet they took me aside and invested in my life as if I were the most important person to them. They believed that God had moved them to be present and available in their immediate sphere of influence, and because of their small, steadfast steps of faithfulness, my life was marked in untold ways—one woman at a time. I'm profoundly grateful. The power of life on life, hidden hospitality.

My heart grieves because I know some of you have never had a woman come alongside you in such a way. You've wanted it. You may have even sought it out, but it never mate-rialized. While we can't change the past, now is our chance to begin that multiplication process. We have the opportunity to be that person for someone else, and I can't wait to see how the Lord will use you. Begin praying about who that person might be.

> If you have had a woman come alongside you and impact your life, share a few memories here. Include the woman's name, along with one or two things you learned from her.

DAY 2

The Unnamed Girl

While one aha moment occurred over that multiplication problem, another jumped out when I unearthed 2 Kings 5:1-4, four verses in Scripture that I'd overlooked before.

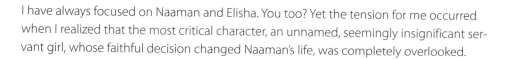

Read 2 Kings 5:1-15, and identify the main characters.

I have always focused on Naaman and Elisha. You too? Yet the tension for me occurred when I realized that the most critical character, an unnamed, seemingly insignificant servant girl, whose faithful decision changed Naaman's life, was completely overlooked.

It just doesn't seem fair, does it? It's easy not to recognize her role because people rarely talk about her. She's not mentioned again, and instead of her courageous actions receiving the fanfare I think she deserves, her character quietly slipped behind the scenes while others became the prominent feature.

In a season of personal discontentment, these obscure verses—2 Kings 5:1-4,15—became a beacon of hope to my frazzled soul. As a young mom with little ones underfoot, the monotony of my hours closed in. Instead of viewing the daily rhythms God had gifted me with as an opportunity to surrender and become transformed through faith, I grew weary in doing small things well and lost heart (Gal. 6:9).

Everything was so very daily. My choices felt unseen, invisible, seemingly insignificant. I tried to remind myself that throughout Scripture the Lord delights in everyday obedience. But I struggled to believe it when I was slogging through mundane moments, asking myself, *Do they really have to eat again? I just made lunch.* Some days success meant nailing the three biggies—food, clothing, and shelter—in any form. Banana dipped in peanut butter for dinner? That counts as fruit and protein; sure honey, we're good.

While you may not be in the throes of toddler tantrums, all of us have felt the pull of wondering, *Lord, how can You use me? Certainly You've called me to more than this?*

You may be stuck right now, wondering why the Lord hasn't opened doors in your everyday life.

Could it be that His door looks profoundly different from what you've anticipated? It may already be open, but you need to walk through it. That's when the Lord used 2 Kings 5:1-4 to prick my heart and adjust my lens of expectation to finally anticipate those unseen moments in light of God's redemption plan. When I fully comprehended the magnitude of the unnamed girl's role, this passage became my personal ministry model.

In this day and age when Facebook notifies us of every accomplishment and accolade, every gathering and gala, it's time to put a face to the unseen. Where we see failure, God sees opportunity. Where we assume weakness, He thrives on giving strength. Where we see insignificant choices, He sees grand possibilities.

Today we seek to celebrate a movement of faithful women who serve in private places, who embrace invisible moments that make an eternal impact. Those servant leaders who no one ever knows about and who never garner praise—they are my role models.

Everything in me wants to lay out all my findings right now so that your excitement can match mine as we journey this together, but I'd be robbing you of that element of surprise as the Lord reveals His truths to your own heart. I've gone over and over this short passage, and the deeper I dig, and the more I pray about how it applies to my own life, the more passionate I become about its message.

It's critical that you know as much about Naaman's situation as possible so that you can understand why my hearts stirs so much for the unnamed girl in verses 1-4.

> Look again at 2 Kings 5:1-15, and jot down what we can determine about Naaman.
> His position:
>
> His popularity:
>
> His problems:
>
> Now let's look at what happened when Naaman sought healing.
> The promise to him (v. 10):
>
> His pride (vv. 11-12):
>
> His proclamation (v. 15):

There are a lot of truths we can pull from this passage, aren't there? Now you understand why most discussions focus on Naaman's healing at Elisha's command, but that is not what I want to focus on today. I couldn't be more excited to introduce you to my role model, and while I'd love to give a formal introduction, her name is never noted.

> Aram had gone on raids and brought back from the land of Israel a young girl who served Naaman's wife.
> 2 KINGS 5:2

Out of all the powerful women in the Bible, I know some of you are wondering why I'd choose a girl we know so little about as my role model. Trust me, we know more than you'd think. It takes extra digging.

Review this chart, observing the contrasts between Naaman and the young girl. Note any differences that stand out to you.

NAAMAN	UNNAMED SERVANT GIRL
Gentile	Hated Jew
Important, great man	Subservient, young girl
Commander of the army	Captive slave in enemy territory
Proud leader	Humble
Easily vocal	Risked life by speaking out

Look over those differences. Isn't that just like God? He bypassed the most expected vessels and instead used the power of one unnamed, insignificant slave girl to change the life of Naaman. Never underestimate divine appointments forged among the ordinary. It's in those moments that God showcases His glory and allows His power to be proclaimed in mighty ways.

I jumped ahead. I couldn't help it. As we set the original scene, it will help to unpack how God moved through this ordinary girl in miraculous ways.

Read verse 2 again.

Here's the reality of that simple sentence: a hostile army from Aram—modern-day Syria—plundered through Israel and ripped a young girl from her family as a spoil of war.

> What do you imagine was going through the young girl's mind as she served Naaman's wife each day?

Verse 2 takes on new meaning now, doesn't it? One thing I want us to take from this passage is that God has a purpose for our pain.

While I can't begin to imagine the terror that her family went through, I know it was God who arranged for this young girl to become a member of Naaman's household. He had a reason for that trial:

> From one man he has made every nationality to live over the whole earth and has determined their appointed times and the boundaries of where they live.
> **ACTS 17:26**

There is nothing that happens in this world by mere chance. God knows every detail in our lives, and in His sovereignty, He has a reason for the difficult times. He is always working to make us more like Him.

We can't imagine the larger picture amidst the anguish, but as we step back, we see why God may have directed this young girl to Naaman's home.

> What do you think was the reason?

That unnamed servant girl became the critical link in the chain of events which led not only to Naaman's leprosy being healed, but also to his bold declaration denouncing past idolatry and proclaiming only one God in all of Israel. This culturally-insignificant slave doing everyday, mundane work changed one very significant man's life. And even now her story is still pointing people to the one true God.

Doesn't that give you chills? Sometimes God Himself takes us to a place we'd never willingly enter so that His radiant image can be forged upon our souls. As we emerge from that dark place, we can reflect His glory by shining in ways that we could never have previously imagined.

In the midst of our most difficult struggles, our loneliness, our feelings of insignificance, our mess becomes the cornerstone of our message—and He uses it in powerful ways. As we invite people into our hearts and homes, often this message will be the vehicle He uses to connect our stories.

> Maybe you're facing a difficult situation right now. How can you see Him working even in the midst of it?

While the Lord is intimately acquainted with our hearts' cries, often the reason He allows for our trial is concealed.

I'm in the middle of one of those seasons right now. I want to know why. My heart's slashed open, my mind plays hard conversations on repeat as I struggle for rest, and I desperately desire to be on the other side of the pain. I need answers, but I don't have them.

In these moments when we feel unseen and unworthy, fearful and lonely, broken and defeated, unwanted and uninvited, He sees, He knows, and He understands.

Without purpose to my pain, there would be no room for this exercise in faith and patience, empathy and forgiveness. I seek to intertwine praise amidst my grief and chase glimmers of unspeakable joy while my soul swirls in sorrow. I know He is "the same yesterday, today, and forever" (Heb. 13:8), so I ask God to use my lonely place.

I have experienced God's faithfulness more times than I can count, and He always remains true. And then I think back on the unnamed girl. She probably felt that same mingling of emotions.

She said to her mistress, "If only my master were with the prophet who is in Samaria, he would cure him of his skin disease."
2 KINGS 5:3

Think that through. She had been kidnapped and was working as Naaman's slave.

> **What would your reaction be if you found out your enemy was ill with an incurable disease?**

I'm not proud to admit it, but my flesh might have triumphed over giving grace, because the old cliché, "you get what you deserve," sprung to my mind.

> **Instead of harboring bitterness against her captor, how did she respond?**

I can't even imagine the grief and despair she felt. From her loneliness, I expected her to sink to low places. And she did. She bent a knee to the One who could redeem her situation. She didn't allow bitterness to destroy her, but she used her loneliness to lead others to Him. She had every legitimate reason to use her circumstances as an excuse to sit this next round out, but she didn't. She offered a cure.

> **While it seems nothing will stop our girl, think about her position and what that means in this historical context as a female slave. Do you think what she did was risky? Why or why not?**

Can't you hear their shock? *How dare this slave make such a ludicrous statement! How could she suggest that a despised prophet be able to cure this sickness when all our best physicians could not?*

She believed and risked it all as she walked out her faith in a proactive and tangible way. Her lack of position, her insecurities, and the possible punishment she might receive for pointing to the one true God, the God of Israel—none of those deterred her from stepping out and declaring truth.

So what was the recourse from her speaking out (v. 4)?

I needed to sit down for this one. They *listened* to her! Powerful people heeded the advice of a lowly servant. This became the link in the chain of events that eventually brought about Naaman's healing.

What character qualities do you think the young girl exhibited that caused them to listen to her?

I imagine she was faithful in the little things. I envision that she was steadfast, loyal, and reliable in her duties, while serving her mistress with honor and respect. She must have modeled compassion, empathy, humility, and love. I assume she was a good listener, because she was aware of the difficulties in the home and embraced an opportunity to turn her words into God-honoring conversation at the most critical and appropriate time. She must have guarded her mistress's reputation and avoided gossip; otherwise her words would not have been received and passed on to Naaman.

Because of this undervalued, unnamed girl's faithfulness, the commander of the king's army was led to confess,

> I know there's no God in the whole world except in Israel. Therefore, please accept a gift from your servant.
> **2 KINGS 5:15**

Do you see why she's my role model?

Sweet friend, that is us. We are that unnamed girl.

Do we want to do something great for God? Then let's embrace the power of one. The beauty that stems from life-on-life, one-on-one relationships never gets old. When our culture screams bigger, better, smarter, stronger, faster, more famous, it's really difficult to see smaller as significant and slower as sanctified, to invite invisibility as a framework for His availability.

That's why I spent so much time getting to know our unnamed girl. She inspires me. We have the privilege of being a part of that life-giving multiplication process. *You* are that someone God wants to use now to impact this generation and the next. *Your* unique gifts, *your* untold story, *your* broken and mended heart, *your* fierce love, *your* brave authenticity—all those intricate threads woven together create the very tapestry He wants to use to unveil His love to someone who needs to experience it.

God chose to use one overlooked servant girl's faithfulness to impact generations for His glory.

Has her story inspired you that becoming a woman of significance doesn't start with a microphone, stage, or even a social media following? It doesn't depend on special talents or a larger-than-life personality. It begins by simply saying, *Yes, Lord, I'm willing and available. Here's my one door, my one table, my one sofa. Use them.*

Small offerings, given with great love, matter.

You are right where He wants you. Just open the door.

DAY 3

The Purposes of Hospitality

Yesterday, we explored how the obedience of one unnamed servant girl led to healing, and ultimately, to God's glory.

I recently heard a story that reminded me of the power of one. One woman was asked to give a reason for her hope (1 Pet. 3:15), and through the power of the Holy Spirit, her answer to that question helped a couple meet Jesus. They went on to tell others, multiplying God's work, just like that multiplication problem from earlier this week.

> Have you experienced something similar? Put to words how you came to know Jesus. Try to remember as many specific people as you can who took the time to tell you about Him.

How do these stories stir me on in my quest for intentional, open-door living? If I'm reminded of the main principles of hospitality—loving Him, loving His will, and following His will into loving others—then I acknowledge and embrace again how intentionally Jesus focused on impacting one person (or small group of people) at a time.

If I apply this in my own life, any pressure of performance fades because He welcomes small, steady steps of faithfulness. When I'm living on mission and I view wherever God has me today with whatever I am doing as the most important place to invite others to experience the love and grace of Christ, then I'm strategically in line with the purpose and calling He's set forth for me. I'm not saying this is always easy, but continually applying a verse from Colossians to my life is helping me:

> Set your minds on things above, not on earthly things.
> **COLOSSIANS 3:2**

> How can you cultivate a habit of focusing your mind on God, allowing Him to work through your daily schedule? Be specific to your calendar and obligations.

Since the basic principles of hospitality are simple to understand, maybe the three purposes of hospitality and Christlike interaction are as well. As I observed how Jesus engaged with those around Him, three primary purposes emerged.

How would you sum up the first purpose of hospitality, based on the following verses?

1. _____

Romans 12:12-13

Romans 15:32

1 Thessalonians 5:11

1 Timothy 5:10

Hebrews 10:25

I'll let you peek at my answer. The first purpose of hospitality is to encourage and build up the saints, providing hospitality to fellow believers.

Creating a sacred space for women who love Jesus and desire to link arms and chase Him down together is one of the most precious invitations we can extend. As my hospitality has expanded over the years, I've learned to be a place (both my home as well as my heart) that announces, *Your brokenness is welcome. Your questions, frustrations, and lone-liness are welcome here. Your desperation and doubt are OK.* It's evolved with time, but I've worked really hard at doing that—at giving people a safe landing spot where they can take a deep breath and give themselves permission to acknowledge, "I don't have my act together, but I still want to be together."

This is where we can start with authentically encouraging and building up the body of believers, by giving permission to come as we are, yet choosing to elevate His goodness no matter the circumstances. Allowing the imperfections of our daily lives to strengthen us—a sisterhood of the imperfect—lays the framework for others to be welcomed into our lives, while pointing to the only One who is capable of giving us a solid foundation. (I'd be remiss to leave out that I am still learning the humility it takes to receive that same invitation.)

Now let's look at the second purpose of hospitality. Based on these verses, record what you think the dual purposes might be.

2. _____

Psalm 145:4

Proverbs 13:20

Acts 8:27-31,35

Colossians 1:27-28

Titus 2:3-5

The second purpose of hospitality is discipleship and mentorship. We are to "make disciples" and teach them to obey God (Matt. 28:18-20). Life-on-life mentoring means cheering, encouraging, sharing goals, listening, teaching, and modeling what it means to be a woman of influence in today's culture—and doing it all for His glory.

Have you ever had someone mentor you? Think outside the box—mentorship doesn't have to be a formal activity. Who has poured into your life and taught you to obey God?

How can you invest in someone younger in age or spiritual maturity?

Knowing God is not only the first step in discipleship, but also in understanding our purpose. When we know Him, we desire to make Him known. There are a myriad of creative ways that we can combine our gifts with our calling to advance the kingdom, and walking alongside another believer is one of the most dynamic ways to do that.

The New Testament relationship between Paul and Timothy is a beautiful example that models the importance of mentoring in spreading the gospel and building the church.

Yet it's important to note that Timothy came to a knowledge of deep faith through the instruction and modeling of his grandmother, Lois, and his mother, Eunice (2 Tim. 1:5). Paul's preaching may very well have been the catalyst for conversion. We do not know for certain, but Timothy's mother's and grandmother's faith were surely the on-ramp for a spiritual encounter.

> This model of discipleship reminds me of the opportunities we have both inside and outside our homes to mentor. List those in your sphere of influence who may need someone to walk alongside them in their life with Christ.

Mentoring with kingdom purpose in mind spans generations. Throughout Scripture, we see examples of how the faithfulness of a generation is tested, not just by their own actions, but by the faithfulness of the following generation. In my parenting (and those whom I disciple in my sphere of influence), I remind myself that I am not just mentoring my own children, but my choices and decisions ultimately affect my children's children and their children. Yet, biblical history also reveals that a legacy can be lost in one generation, so I'm convicted and compelled to ask myself tough questions, not just about my own children, but those whose lives intersect with mine as well.

> Take some time to think through these questions this week:
>
> ☐ Who else is pouring into the next generation and for what purpose?
> ☐ How am I passing the baton of faithfulness to the generations of tomorrow?
> ☐ Am I equipping those around me in sound doctrine, apologetics, and a heart-knowledge that points back to His perfect character?
> ☐ Am I raising or influencing culture changers who are willing to stand up for biblical truth in a society that preaches tolerance amidst moral decline?

We're called to pass the baton by equipping the next generation of believers. We have significant opportunities to disciple and lead the generations following us by sharing our time, love, and stories. There's a challenge given in 2 Timothy:

> You have heard me teach things that have been confirmed by many reliable witnesses. Now teach these truths to other trustworthy people who will be able to pass them on to others.
> **2 TIMOTHY 2:2, NLT**

Will you accept the challenge? Name the person God lays on your heart.

For those older women with silver gracing their crowns who have accepted the challenge (and continue to do so), thank you. Thank you for battling for the next generations. I know we can be a tricky bunch. Thank you for not giving up on us, even if we thumb a nose to the wisdom you generously share. I see you prayer warriors, awake before the sun, going before the Father on our behalf. We need you. We need you to mentor us, to remind us that the Bible is all true—every word of it—and that it is worth it. We need you to confront us when we stray from that truth, to share your stories of pain and loss and regret, and to testify to God's ever-sustaining power. Thank you for pointing us to Him.

The final purpose of hospitality we'll look at today leads the way for the other two. Write what you think it may be based on the verses below:

3. _____

Psalm 105:1

Matthew 28:16-20

Romans 1:15-16

The third purpose of hospitality is to proclaim the gospel—to evangelize. Like all of the purposes of hospitality, this is not optional for believers.

The word *evangelism* often paralyzes people because we've turned it into complicated courses with step-by step procedures or associate it with screaming evangelists who've lost their joy. When we demystify its definition—simply spreading the gospel—and agree that the gospel is "the good news" about Jesus, it's easy to begin putting this into practice.

Let's practice. Write here in simple terms the good news of Jesus.

All three of these purposes of hospitality are primarily ministries of example. When Jesus modeled this method of invitation with *follow Me, come with Me, sit with Me,* He emphasized learning first through observation. Through welcoming others into our lives and homes, we open up an environment for relationships to grow, observation to occur, and opportunities to model Christlike responses and obedience.

First Corinthians 3:5-7 reminds us that sharing the good news is often a process, and we are one strong link in the gospel story. While there is power in one person pouring into the life of another person, it is often a team effort to disciple someone throughout a lifetime.

> Think back to who told you about Jesus. Now, list some names of others who have discipled you along the way. Say a little prayer of thanks to God for their obedience in living out the commandments to love others and make disciples.

Often, we won't see the fruit of what we've planted, but we know that our open door is part of the harvest, and God is responsible for the results.

> Where are you called to be faithful in that process now?

How much do you love receiving good news? Why aren't we bursting at the seams not just to share good news, but the greatest news, the sensational news that we are loved with an everlasting love, and we have life filled with more abundance than we can ever imagine? Who doesn't want to learn the amazing news that binds the brokenhearted, releases captives to freedom, and turns strangers and enemies into friends? The good news of the gospel provides a new kind of invitation, which welcomes messy, imperfect people into a life with a perfect Savior. It's grace that chooses to use broken people, heal them, and champion their mess into messages of hope.

That's the invitation I want to share on behalf of a God who's gracious and merciful.

HOSPITALITY INVITATION

Take a few minutes this week to create a spiritual time line of sorts. Think through important life markers, both good and bad. Note those people who impacted you during those times. It might not have been a grandiose gesture. It could have been a friend who sat quietly and listened as you shared struggles or someone who spoke hard truth in love as you floundered through a decision-making process. It may have been a teacher or coach who encouraged you to follow a dream by working hard.

Name at least one person the Lord brought to mind. Today, attempt to track that person down. Can you find them on social media? Are they still in town? Send them a note and express gratitude for investing in you.

Earlier this week, I wrote, "Today we seek to celebrate a movement of faithful women who serve in private places, who embrace invisible moments that make an eternal impact. Those servant leaders who no one ever knows about and who never garner praise—they are my role models."

Let's put a light on the invisible servants today. Take time to thank the women who selflessly make coffee on Sunday mornings; the women rocking babies so you receive a break; the prayer warriors who walk the aisles of your church, praying over every person who will sit in every seat. Who can you encourage and appreciate today?

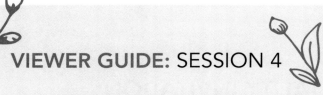

VIEWER GUIDE: SESSION 4

Watch the Session 4 video and discuss with your group the following questions:

1. As you studied this week, did God bring to mind a person who you could mentor/journey/partner with? Tell your group about this person.

2. What simple, everyday steps can you take to begin creating a legacy of welcome in your home?

3. Jen says that creating a legacy of welcome begins with "giving our ordinary moments to the Lord." What might that look like practically in your own life? Is this something you already practice? Or would it be a change for you?

4. Natasha says, "Because of our salvation, God has work for us to do." What work do you think God has for you to do?

5. Natasha says, "The way we see ourselves can be a hindrance sometimes. Our faith walk is not really about us at all. It's about who we serve." How does that resonate with you?

6. Do you strive to be a "safe" person for those around you? What does that mean practically?

Video sessions available for purchase
at LifeWay.com/JustOpenTheDoor

LET'S PUT IT ON THE CALENDAR

WEEK 4:
WHEN HOSPITALITY IS A CHALLENGE

Her statement stunned me, but the truth teller in me appreciated her candor: "Jen, I'm sorry, but there is no magic pill that will suddenly make opening up my home easier. I've never hosted anyone who wasn't in my family. Ever since I was little, I've longed to be one of those girls who could walk into a room, introduce myself to a stranger, and initiate meaningful conversation, but I can't, and I no longer try. I don't invite, but no one invites me either. I'm lonely, but it's easier now, because I have no expectations from anyone, and I can no longer be disappointed."

My heart ached as she shared. Her countenance crushed by years of rejection and fear of failure, yet raw honesty was what I had requested. I didn't want women smiling on the outside while struggling on the inside. I wanted to hear from a few women brave enough to admit their hidden vulnerabilities, because when just one person goes first and verbalizes her struggle, I guarantee she will be the mouthpiece for many more who won't.

For years, my new friend lived in fear of taking that chance and missed out on all that God intended for her. Brick by brick, hurt by hurt, she'd built walls around the door of her heart and home. But as she shared her story about the bondage that kept her from community, glimpses of newfound freedom began to break through.

There was no magic pill to make it easier. I had no simple "1, 2, 3, formula" to share for friendship, but we had lots of discussions about what dying to self means in light of Scripture. We stumbled through the hard question of whether pursuing hospitality is ever optional, and in doing so, we celebrated the fact that no matter our past, a new legacy can begin today.

Hospitality was a challenge for her. It still is, but Christ loves to help us rewrite our stories, and the more we allow Him to guide our hand, the grander it becomes.

I'll never forget the inaugural excitement and wonder she experienced when she invited her neighbors for pizza.

And they said yes!

DAY 1

The Doer, The Doubter, and I Don't Think So

7:30 a.m. arrived quickly that Monday morning.

As the camera crew and the *Just Open the Door* Bible study team arrived at our home, I welcomed the newcomers, and then ran to finish my early morning hostess priority: brew strong coffee and lots of it. (I confess, I was on my third cup.) This day had been on the calendar for months, and at every turn, I'd been bubbling over with a passion to share my insights. It was time to get rolling, and while I was a little nervous since it was my first time teaching directly to camera, I was certain the looming feeling would pass as soon as we started. It never ever crossed my mind what would happen next.

The producer asked, "Jen, are you ready to start?"

"Yep, I think so," I stuttered.

"Everyone ready? Let's get going. 3, 2, 1 Action!" (OK, so he didn't say action, but I've always wanted to experience that.)

Everyone was completely silent per the producer's request. As the cameras started rolling for my first teaching session, I froze—as in, mind blank, stomach sank, scared, completely paralyzed. Never in my years of ministry, of leading worship and teaching, had I experienced a mental shutdown like I did. I'm never at a total loss for words. Well, maybe once in the eighth grade when I had a church solo—back before "cheat" monitors (which now prompt worship leaders with the song words). The musical measures began playing and I could not remember how the song started. At all. No clue. Noticeably uncomfortable for me, sympathetic souls in the audience started eying each other as they wondered how I'd recover. Now decades later, I'm once again that eighth-grade girl, reliving those mortifying moments with the same range of circling emotions. My palms are sweaty just typing this.

> Have you ever experienced something similar? Maybe it was in your public speaking class or practicum. An audition or job interview?

Quite possibly, you've stuttered out words after meeting someone new only to replay them over and over, wondering why you didn't say something different. Most likely, you can recreate the scenario in a heartbeat even after years have gone by.

I wish I could tell you that things improved for me immediately, but it took days to work through these new challenges. I spent the next few weeks assaulted with all the "could've, would've, should've" doubts, and it finally hit me. The anxiety, the amount of work, the wish for a do-over, and the tripping over my tongue, mingled with slicing comparisons swirling in my mind are identical to the emotions and barriers that keep us from opening our door to others. All the insecurities that women have voiced to me are now front and center as I write this and phew, my heart's beating faster on your behalf, because I know the fears and obstacles associated with opening a door are real.

Weeks into this study, your eyes likely have been opened to the critical importance of biblical hospitality. You've realized it's not optional, yet you're not quite sure if you're ready to move out of your comfort zone yet. There are still many lingering doubts and supposed obstacles as to why it doesn't happen. I get it. So this week, let's identify what's holding you back.

After hearing common barriers, I've narrowed it down to three overarching descriptions. You might find yourself in one or two of these, and you may have even verbalized these very excuses. I know I have. While I'm specifically unpacking what keeps us from opening our homes to others, this week's study can be applied to any of the work God intends for us to do.

> Rate yourself on a scale of 1-10 for each of these descriptions, 1 meaning this is not true of me at all and 10 meaning, "Are you reading my diary?"

THE DOER: The thought of adding one more item to my already maxed schedule overwhelms me. I'm held hostage by a crazed calendar of my own making. The hustle and bustle of my everyday life leaves no time to open our home to others, let alone begin creating a legacy of hospitality. My commitments are more important.

1 – – – – – – – – – – – – 5 – – – – – – – – – – – – 10

THE DOUBTER: Inviting people into my home feels like inviting judgment of my entertaining skills. I'm afraid of being exposed for who I really am. I'm good at hiding. I have serious doubts that my house is good enough, decluttered enough, big enough, homey enough. Women compare and judge, and I'll come up short.

I struggle with my conversational ability, and I doubt my personality meshes with inviting people into my home. I doubt they'd even want to come. I am not a good cook, so I doubt anyone would like what I serve. The list goes on.

1 – – – – – – – – – – – – – 5 – – – – – – – – – – – – – 10

I DON'T THINK SO: I really don't think I can do this. I've never had hospitality modeled for me, and I'm not sure where to start. I don't think I have anyone to invite. I've tried and been hurt in the past, and I'm afraid to put myself out there again. I don't think the rejection is worth it, but then I wonder, is the loneliness?

1 – – – – – – – – – – – – – 5 – – – – – – – – – – – – – 10

Which of these three do you identify with the most? Explain.

What lies do you believe? Let's identify the specific struggles that keep us from cultivating a life of hospitality, so we can work to counter them with truth.

Finish the sentences below.

It's hard for me to open my home because . . .

I don't think I'm a very good host because . . .

When it comes to opening our homes, comparison's stranglehold plays games with our self-image. When we build our identity on other's expectations, it rubs against God's view of us.

I've spent a lot of time with our teen daughters discussing our worldview. We all have one: an ideology, philosophy, or theology that provides an overarching approach on how we interpret reality and perceive truth about God, the world, and ultimately how the two interact with each other. What controls our minds controls our choices. Our attitudes and perspectives flow from the heart, so the way we think and act are all determined by what we believe to be true.

As believers, we are faced with two foundational questions, *How do we know what is absolute truth?* and *How do we live our lives in view of what we know to be true?* Believe it or not, our worldview has a direct correlation with how we live out a life of welcome.

In what ways, if any, do you believe the above statement to be true of you and your worldview?

In what ways, if any, is it not true of you?

We all have a choice that stems from who God says we are and how we are to live. We know our identities as women of God who are abundantly, radically, and ridiculously loved by Him, and we acknowledge His command to pursue hospitality. So here's our simple choice: We either declare that we will be a host or a hostage. We wave our flag today, identifying that as His disciples we step forward and live lives of welcome or we're held hostage by our hangups and the opinions of others.

> Do not remember the past events,
> pay no attention to things of old.
> Look, I am about to do something new;
> even now it is coming. Do you not see it?
> Indeed, I will make a way in the wilderness,
> rivers in the desert.
> **ISAIAH 43:18-19**

To experience freedom in your hospitality, what do you need to put behind you?

Last week, I provided frozen pizzas and ice cream for a teen activity. The next day a "helpful" friend felt I should know that in trying to model servant-like hospitality, they'd appreciate if all food was homemade. Apparently, I was the only one to provide store-bought food.

While I do believe that we honor our guests through investing time and effort with special gifts of love and service, please reject the lie that somehow the heart of hospitality is linked with the food we serve, our home's décor, or factors that are often out of our control. I almost let her steal my joy over pizza for teens. Quite frankly, if the miraculous feeding of the five thousand happened right now and the boy's offering was his pizza and ice cream, I'm making a leap, but I think the Lord would have gladly received it.

It took me two days to wrestle down this ugly mixture of anger, comparison, and failure that had seeped into my soul from one simple text (and I'm the one writing the book on hospitality). I had to choose hostage or host. That's why our biblical worldview is so critical, because the war on our feelings affects our freedom to open our homes. Change will come if we truly desire Him to do something new through us.

As I type this, it all sounds so simple, but the reality is that it's a day in, day out battle to realign facts over feelings. Our feelings, though valuable gifts that help us experience life, are notoriously horrible captains. If we allow altered emotions to steer us, it's a crash waiting to happen. Wholeheartedly loving God and believing the truth requires that we anchor our feelings in His Word and keep careful watch over what fills our hearts and minds. Only with hearts fully alive in Him, ones that dance in the freedom He offers and celebrate this abundant life as people who live loved, can we live out this call to action.

Some days it's much harder than others, like the day our then 10-year-old daughter realized our floors weren't quite up to par.

"Mom, when are we replacing our floors? They're tacky. You know they are."

She'd overheard a conversation with a friend who mentioned our welcoming home, but added that she hoped we'd be able to replace our tacky floors soon. Yep, my friend voiced that word, and now my daughter couldn't shake it. Quite frankly, neither could I. Every time I tripped on the ripped linoleum piece, that sneaky whisper echoed, "Jen, everyone notices your tacky floors." I was tempted to shut my door.

Did she realize the angst she stirred within my soul? I'd spent years choosing to be content with the state of my home: reconciling the fixes and updates that needed to be done with the command to pursue hospitality.

Oh friend, when we least expect it, the enemy of our souls (disguised as comparison) sneaks up like a thief and attempts to rob us of all joy, especially when we're inviting others into the very places we are most vulnerable: our homes, our hearts, our stories.

A thief comes only to steal and kill and destroy. I have come so that they may have life and have it in abundance.
JOHN 10:10

Do you believe that the enemy will use every tactic to steal your joy, to overwhelm and distract you from opening your life to others? Why or why not? What tactics does he attempt with you?

In Galatians 1:10, Paul didn't mince words when he questioned the Galatian church. What did he ask?

Paul was directly warning them about the dangers found in abandoning essential doctrine and leaning toward a corrupted gospel. He highlighted a direct correlation between our motives that stem from pride and approval from others and a skewed theology.

Have you ever thought of it in those terms? When we fall prey to comparison, how does it corrupt our doctrine surrounding hospitality and our ability to extend an invitation?

My daughter looked to me for how I'd respond to our tacky floors. How did I model where I put my worth? Did I want her hope to be hung on what our house looked like or her value anchored in the truth of who God says she is?

Romans 15 reflects what I desire my outlook to be about my home:

Now may the God of hope fill you with all joy and peace as you believe so that you may overflow with hope by the power of the Holy Spirit.
ROMANS 15:13

I want her to see a mom whose pure and simple faith embraces the fullness of God's unending, overflowing, abundant, and perfect love. She will know that our lives have been so changed, that we can't help but tell others what the Savior has been up to. We can't help but invite them into our home because our tacky floors tell so many stories of His goodness.

Right then and there, I declared that I would not let something as silly as a comment about my floors steal from me the sweet blessing of community I craved—nor my responsibility and privilege as a Christ-follower to multiply that joy with as many people as possible.

In Psalm 18:30, we're assured that God's "way is perfect; the word of the LORD is pure," so I refused to allow my delight in welcoming others disintegrate because of the insecurities swirling in my head. When my eyes gravitated toward the things in our home that needed work, I chose to change my perspective with a record of hope.

Those tacky floors welcomed guests from cities and countries around the world. Those tacky floors invited children to wrestle and giggle and build forts on top of them. Those tacky floors were where thousands of feet had walked during hundreds of gatherings. Those tacky floors had both celebrated new life and supported the hearts of mourners. Those tacky floors had witnessed so much grace in action, all while refusing to disclose the secrets they heard. Those tacky floors had told stories of a life well spent.

Could any model home really replace what I loved so much about those floors? I sat our daughter down on our tacky floors and pointed out the wear and tear.

"You see that tear in the vinyl? You crawled for the first time over that spot. And that stain? Remember when Lola got into the chocolate, and we thought she might die? The Lord took care of your special puppy, and that stain reminds us of that. See this coffee spot? It reminds me of the night it got there, a really special evening when my friends and I were crying and giggling together, assuring each other we could make it through our exhausting days. It's OK to think about buying new floors. I think about it too, but for now, I want you to love them and all they symbolize. They stand for life. Life to the fullest."

And thinking now of this moment with my daughter reminds me of that subtle one-word perspective shift we've talked about: We never *have* to celebrate tacky floors; we *get* to. Yes, they're messy, just like we are. But there's something awfully beautiful in that.

Also, after sixteen years, I finally got new floors. They're beautiful.

DAY 2

Margin

Every wise woman builds her house, but a foolish one tears it down
with her own hands.
PROVERBS 14:1

Perhaps all of us want a beautiful, cozy home to welcome others into. Before guests
arrive we light a candle, clear the clutter, gather our favorite comfort foods, and anxiously
anticipate time together. With soft music playing in the background, we envision the ideal
evening setting, but a seemingly beautiful house crumbles if built on a foundation of poor
choices, negative attitudes, and stress-filled living.

A wise woman creates a home that elevates Jesus and others to their rightful positions
before herself. We are the thermostat in our homes, and we set the temperature for our
family and friends. Setting the temperature begins with priorities.

When I walk through the process of helping women with their finances, I have them
observe their monthly calendar, daily schedule, and financial expenses. Then I ask what
they think about this statement: Our calendars and our receipts tell us what we need to
know about where our priorities lie and what we value most.

Would you say this statement is true for you? Why or why not?

I request that they systematically track every penny spent over the course of a few weeks.
For a free spirit like me, using the word *budget* is like nails on a chalkboard, but giving
every dollar a job (assigning each dollar a specific task) is tremendously valuable. Rather
than letting money control your decisions, you're actively taking control back. Life may still
be a bit stressful with money a little tight, but if you anticipate it, your finances shouldn't
send you into a perpetual state of panic. It really works!

What if you applied this same principal to your schedule in order to get your priorities
back under your control? If you don't have margin in your schedule, you create a shifting
foundation, and hospitality will be the last thing you pursue. Because no matter how we
attempt to excuse it, spin it, or dress it up, our calendars call out our priorities.

What does your calendar currently say about your priorities?

What would you like it to say?

Control is an illusion. When my mother-in-law was diagnosed with a brain tumor, she was given weeks to live. With that kind of prognosis, a bucket list becomes pretty small and a person's priorities get realigned instantaneously.

I have a box of conversation starters on our table, and one of them asks a question my mother-in-law had to answer. Answer it below.

If you had one week to live, how would you spend your time?

Turn to 1 Peter 4:7-11. Peter gave his own prognosis when he announced to the believers that "the end of all things is near" (v. 7). What did Peter say to do in the last days?

Were you shocked with his response? If so, which part surprised you the most?

Verse 8 says, "Above all, love each other deeply" (NIV). Specifically, what two ways are we to live this out (v. 9)?

If you had any doubt as to the importance of showing hospitality, I hope this sealed the deal for you. If I said to you, "The world is ending soon. What are you going to do?" you likely would not reply, "I'm going to show hospitality." Yet here it is. Our answer without question. Open your door. Invest in others. Create margin for pursuing hospitality so that God may be glorified.

We have a chance for a do-over moment right now. The idea of getting a clean slate? A fresh start? After all the ways I can mess things up? Bring it on, because our time is finite with no guarantees for tomorrow.

I'm living my do-over. About five years ago, busy had become my habit. With five children, overscheduled, overwhelmed, and no margin carved into daily life, busy became my fallback and my downfall. I said yes when I should have said no. When no one stepped up, I was your go-to girl. Busy became a badge of honor laced with bondage, one that certainly didn't garner praise from those who matter most. While my priorities were all "good" things, they were out of line, and my choices affected everyone around me.

Some of you understand. You're overwhelmed, tightly wound, tears stay close to the surface, and the do-good, try-hard, dizzy busy life you've created steals your joy, winds you up, and spits you out until you've spun out of control.

What I needed, and what you likely need, is grace. Grace for this one moment to settle your soul. Grace for yourself and your soon-to-be noes—because you realize something has got to change, right?

God is providing us a humble, grace-filled, and powerful way to redeem our time—margin. It's the antidote to our overwhelmed souls. It's that space that exists between our normal load and our outer limits. Margin is our breathing room. It's the place where our souls camp between the weary and worn out, where we rest and connect with our Creator. We spend time with Him, so He can pour into us, and only then can we pour out.

Maybe you're overwhelmed and barely keeping your head above water, or perhaps you've got huge chunks of your calendar open every day but you aren't spending that time serving others or showing hospitality. No matter what season you're in, Scripture will help you examine your next steps.

Read Proverbs 14:8, and rewrite the verse in your own words.

A person's true identity is forged in the inconveniences of every day. To love God is to love His will. That's how a wise woman builds a beautiful home.

Often God asks us to interrupt our best-laid plans so that His will can be manifested, and we'll give an account for our seemingly small choices (Rom. 14:12). I knew that I'd reached a boiling point when those simple inconveniences seemed insurmountable. I stepped back and examined my priorities in how they aligned to God's Word.

Have you taken time out to evaluate your schedule?

On a scale from 1-10, how busy are you throughout the week? Do you have time to extend an invitation? Is margin available to allow for interruptions?

Does your schedule belong to Him? In our jump, run, repeat, frazzled lifestyle, *balance* is a buzzword used without implementation. Have you been purposeful in your planning?

What can you do this week to create more margin or to use your margin wisely, serving others and showing hospitality?

I began by creating room to breathe again. Practically, I looked at my calendar and began to assess my activities. I asked myself what constituted as life-giving and included an opportunity to point others to Him and which choices stole our family's joy, energy, and quality time. If prior obligations couldn't be canceled, I looked to turn them into opportunities for meaningful encounters and focused on being faithful with the small things I'd been given to do. I learned to ask myself, *How is this benefiting my family?* If it's not, then I put it on the short list. I fought for margin and then guarded that extra space like it was my job.

When I evaluate where to account for my time, I ask myself, *Does this align with my purpose as a Christ follower? Is my decision laced with any people-pleasing tendencies? How does it impact my relationship with the Lord, my husband, and my family?* If those questions are answered, then I can begin reaching out to my surrounding spheres of influence and add additional responsibilities. I want no regrets.

Without margin, we aren't available. It's in the margin that God sweeps in and does His most powerful work. Hospitality lives in the margin, in the unexpected moments when we release our own agenda to the One who's greater. It's in that margin we find inexhaustible grace for this exhausted and overachieving world.

> Read the following verses and jot down how they might be used as a litmus test for the way we use our time.
> Colossians 3:17
>
> Luke 16:10

I love this quote from Elisabeth Elliot's *Passion and Purity:*

> *If we hold tightly to anything given to us, unwilling to let it go when the time comes to let it go or unwilling to allow it to be used as the Giver means it to be used, we stunt the growth of the soul. It is easy to make a mistake here, "If God gave it to me," we say, "it's mine. I can do what I want with it." No. The truth is that it is ours to thank Him for and ours to offer back to Him, ours to relinquish, ours to lose, ours to let go of—if we want to find our true selves, if we want real Life, if our hearts are set on glory.[1]*

Practically, I began to intentionally offer my time back to Him. In our family, we slashed the overabundance of kids' activities to have more focused family time. We switched sports obligations to keep the Sabbath holy. I evaluated work and ministry opportunities through a new lens.

More importantly, I intentionally included margin into my schedule so I could be more missional about opening our door. The Lord began shifting my mind-set from one of irritated interruptions to that of initiating invitation. Generosity of my time began to look a whole lot more like Jesus, and I realized once again that slowing down and creating true space for others means more than opening our homes. It starts with opening our hearts, which pours into an open calendar, which in turn makes room for our neighbors. Again, we come full circle to His Greatest Commandment: loving Him and loving others (Matt. 22:36-40). He's the best designer for a beautiful homelife. Being a doer alongside Him is the only way to get it done.

DAY 3

Our Calling

As I've studied these passages this week, I've been preaching to myself. Sometimes we just need to give ourselves a good talking to, along with the reminder that we are "a new creation" in Christ (2 Cor. 5:17). Because while I believe that we have the power to replace lies with truth and throw old, sinful patterns to the curb, sometimes that sin nature tries its best to claw its way back, doesn't it? Living in freedom is a day in, day out choice to renew our minds, especially when our goal is a legacy of hospitality in a setting as vulnerable as our home.

I shared with my friend Diane that I'd been so caught up in all the "doing and doubting" that I hadn't been mindful to choose joy amidst my appointed work. I woke up to a text that included this reminder when I needed it:

> Now to him who is able to do above and beyond all that we ask or think according to the power that works in us.
> EPHESIANS 3:20

"The power that works in us." This is the answer to our doubts, excuses, inadequacies, fears, and any other barriers that hinder us from leaning into what He asks us to do: His power at work in us! Not mine. I don't know about you, but I'm clinging to that truth like it's the last life vest left between me and the Bermuda Triangle. Without His power in us, sharing our story and pursuing hospitality can seem impossible.

In week 2, we talked about the Word being alive and active. I noted that the root for active was *energeō*.

Do you remember the English comparison? Write out some of the definitions. (Hint: The Greek version looks a lot like our English version.)

Note where it's used in 1 Thessalonians 2:

> This is why we constantly thank God, because when you received the word of God that you heard from us, you welcomed it not as a human message, but as it truly is, the word of God, which also works effectively [*energeo*] in you who believe.
> **1 THESSALONIANS 2:13**

Do you realize what is available to us? Jesus' life-giving, bondage-breaking, fear-crushing, faith-building, door-opening power is at work in us for those who believe. I need to camp out on that for a minute. If you sat across from me, you'd witness a woman who's writing scared and exposed. With tears streaming down my face, my heart's slayed open—real, raw, vulnerable—certain that the Lord has me confused with someone else, because I'm unqualified, unworthy, and unequipped for this task.

"I don't think I can do this," I cried. And here's the reality: I can't. You can't. But *He* can.

His power is our life source. Somewhere along the way, we started assuming we need to control this. That opening our home is easier if we try harder, create more, calm down, clean up. That if we keep striving in our own power, eventually it will fall into place. But in reality, we begin to fall apart.

That's why it's so reassuring that Scripture is filled with messy stories of imperfect people made whole by the Master. They couldn't accomplish a lick of good on their own, but with His power alive and infused in them they shaped generations for Him.

I dare you to show me where in Scripture it says, "You're scared? You're nervous? You're out of your comfort zone? Oh, then don't bother. I need someone better." Nope, never. Through His grace and favor God sees fit to use us when we're completely and unequivocally unworthy and unqualified for the task.

Can we all take a deep breath?

In fact, God always uses people in process, so when it comes to hospitality, let's raise our hands high and say, "I'm your girl." My attitude is in process. My house sure is in process. My laundry is in process (24 years and counting). My kids are in process, and my cooking is in process too.

What are things that are "in process" for you? What have you used as an excuse not to open your door?

Read Luke 10:25-37.

When God laid out the Greatest Commandment and gave the example of the good Samaritan, I didn't see any "If, then" statement. Jesus gave no qualifiers. He didn't command, *If you feel loved, if you feel like you measure up, if your kids are behaving well, then you can go and do likewise.* Yet that's how many approach this.

He simply stated,

> Go and do the same.
> **LUKE 10:37**

God's got this and He's got you too.

He's never made a promise He hasn't kept.

Read the following verses and write down what they tell us God does when He calls us.

2 Corinthians 3:5

Hebrews 13:20-21

Philippians 2:13

Ephesians 2:10

When God calls us, He qualifies us, equips us, and prepares us to do what He has called us to do.

> Fill in your own. "When He calls me, He will _____
> _____."

Friend, all week we've talked about the truth of who we are in Christ and the power available to us. I pray you're ending today with hope. I sure am. It was the exact reminder I needed. But we still have to choose to change. We can spend our whole lives hiding behind our doubts, our busyness, our pride, our "I don't think so" attitude and miss out on the joy and honor of seeing how God uses someone so unqualified to build an inviting home full of peace, hope, and love.

You still have a choice to daily open your door to God's truth, His love, and those He wants to love through you. What will you choose?

HOSPITALITY INVITATION

Oh sweet friend, we've come so far in this past month. We've laid a foundation for the importance of Jesus' heart for inviting and welcoming. We've seen how He models the continuous pursuit of others around Him. I truly believe this week enables a breakthrough to a greater freedom than we've known before. We lay down our excuses, our anxiety, our calendars, our need for control and we humbly ask the Lord, "What do You have for me to do in living a life of welcome?"

Flip back to the beginning pages where you noted your perception of hospitality and those things that potentially kept you from opening your heart and home to others. Has anything changed yet? (Don't worry, there's still time.)

Examine your calendar and pray over where He might have you carve out space on a consistent basis to walk this road of welcome.

I've been thinking a lot about comparison this week, and I've made this my prayer. Won't you join me?

Father, renew my mind. Think for me and through me until Your thoughts are my thoughts. Speak into me and speak out of me until my words sound like Yours. Pour over me Your righteousness, so that my heart mimics Your heart. Assure me that my identity is found only in You—that my worth does not come from my home, my job, my family, my prestige, my spiritual fervor, or my accomplishments—for none of these can fill an emptiness that only You can. My hope is found only in You.

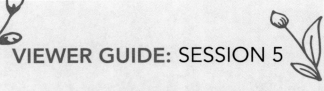

VIEWER GUIDE: SESSION 5

Watch the Session 5 video and discuss with your group the following questions:

1. Read Matthew 19:26. When have you felt God has told you to do something that seems impossible?

2. Why do you think money is mentioned so often in the Bible?

3. What expectations of opening up your door do you need to let go of in order to live out our call to be hospitable?

4. Nicki says, "Martha struggled with priorities over presence." How have you struggled with limited hospitality like Martha?

5. Do you know your neighbors—the ones who literally live next door, in front of, or behind you? If not, how can you get to know them? Together, think of ways to have a "fun street."

6. What is a baby step you can take today to begin to open your door to others?

Video sessions available for purchase
at LifeWay.com/JustOpenTheDoor

PULL
UP A
CHAIR

WEEK 5:

AT THE TABLE

As I held a smudged, handwritten recipe for easy chicken enchiladas, memories from my carefree days as a 16-year-old catapulted back to the present. I remember Jan—a fun, young mom—who took four other high school girls and me under her wing. During a time in our lives when school, friends, boys, and parents triggered hours of emotional dumping—cloaked as discussion and dialogue—our weekly home gatherings served as a buoy keeping us afloat. A time when affirmation was currency and attention was the payment.

But then she tweaked our typical Bible study time by adding some cooking lessons. Each week, she introduced us to new foods, new cooking techniques, and new kitchen tips.

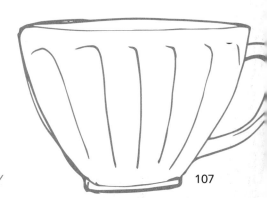

It definitely wasn't like your grandma's Bible study, although she took one of life's most simple pleasures from that bygone era—learning to cook from scratch—and intertwined it into foundational truths.

Every week she picked one meal for us to master—a main dish, side, and dessert. And as we chopped and mixed, folded and kneaded, not only did it awaken our creativity, but it allowed conversation to flow untethered by the constraints of a typical discipleship time.

As we chopped the veggies, she shared on the "dicey-ness" of marriage and the importance of putting time into making a marriage a true partnership. As we stirred, she shared wisdom on the swirling challenges of parenting. Then, as the desserts baked, we'd come to the table and talk about typical stresses we dealt with as senior-high students, while she led us to Scriptures to help combat peer pressure.

As weeks went by, we learned the art of appreciating simple ingredients—how they're useless by themselves, but when blended with other unimportant elements, a simple fare becomes a feast. We learned to slow down, to realize no matter how much we wanted to rush the process and race to the end, the joy was found in the journey. By embracing the process, even when it resulted in a few burned edges from mistakes made along the way, the end result was always worth the wait. Isn't that just like life?

Jesus prioritized time around the table because He understood the power it represents—the holy moments, the sensory ties, the significance of meals intertwined with gatherings.

Jan followed Jesus' lead as she wove discipleship and evangelism into the fabric of a unique hospitality experience and fed both our bodies and our souls. Those summer months together weren't necessarily about exchanging deep theological takeaways, but we all left with something even better: a safe place to learn and create, an open home where our hearts were heard, and a shared rite of passage—one generation equipping the next through tangible life skills that decades later now serve my own family well.

This week, let's come to the table and feast on so much more than good food.

DAY 1

The Importance of Table Time

While serving as a college resident advisor, I realized one of the easiest ways to build a bridge to friendships was through serving food and gathering around the table. My job required me to get to know the girls on my hall, and I needed to find the quickest way to create meaningful companionship and connection. With only a few dollars to purchase supplies and no real oven access, I began by making popcorn and Rice Krispies Treats® in the dorm microwave and inviting the girls to my makeshift "table," perfectly situated under my lofted bunk beds.

Let's be honest, nothing quite says "welcome" to lonely, freshmen girls who are struggling to find friends more than a mixture of marshmallows, peanut butter, chocolate, and late-night conversation. They came in droves, because food welcomes in ways that words can't.

But there was always one girl who didn't come. Every once in a while I brought my "treats on the go," knocked on her door, and offered a listening ear to a precious but private girl who wasn't quite acclimating to her new environment. It always involved goodies, because food paves a path I can't.

What I learned during those years was that while food is obviously a means for satisfying hunger, gathering "at the table" is so much more than feeding our tummies. It's an opening to our hearts. It holds the power to revolutionize the way families and friends connect, to touch the soul in a new way, because everything is deeper at the table. Community's sweeter, laughter's louder, stories are richer, and heartache's heavier.

Long before the Internet or Facebook, the table was the first and most important social platform ever built. Gathering around the table has been at the epicenter of relationships long before any of us hosted our first meal. A meeting place for connection and belonging, the table has always been a distinct marker in kingdom building.

Jesus understood this more than anyone because He knows how deep our hunger runs. Physical and spiritual nourishment intertwine, and Jesus could provide for them both.

Jesus invited others to a meal and gathered around food more than any other fellowship activity in Scripture. He modeled tangible opportunities for spiritual growth to occur around the table and demonstrated that food and table fellowship go hand in hand because they point to a similar purpose: life.

Think through what you know about Jesus' ministry on earth. List any times you remember a table or food being involved. (It's OK if you can't think of any right now—we'll be reading some together.)

It should be no surprise that just as we've witnessed how the theology of hospitality began in the garden and ended in Revelation with a great feast, it makes sense that a similar theology of food and fellowship runs symmetrically throughout Scripture.

Read Genesis 2:8-9 and Revelation 22:1-2, then fill in the blanks:

God created the world and began by furnishing _____ and ended it with a _____, yielding twelve different crops.

God even made us with ten thousand taste buds to enjoy our food. (Thank You, Lord, for caring about this detail!)

If we break it down even further, some of His first and last instructions implied to eat and drink freely.

Take a guess as to how many references there are to the act of eating (not including drinking and food or references to meals that are indirect) in Scripture.

More than seven hundred!

The imagery of eating laces itself throughout Scripture perhaps more beautifully than any other example.

As you continue studying Scripture, note when invitations to enter a home are extended or when you observe the mention of breaking of bread, cup, drink, eating "before the Lord," reclining at the table, anointing with oil, and food or handwashing because they imply table fellowship as well.

Look up the following passages, and note what food or table the passage refers to and the purpose of them.
Exodus 16:13-17

Exodus 25:23-30

Psalm 23:5

John 21:12-19

Revelation 22:17

God understands the substance food brings to both body and soul. As we explore the scope of how often the act of eating together spanned both the Old and New Testaments, I'm more convinced that gathering around food is one of the most effective tools to welcome others into community. It makes me all the more fervent about including simple offerings of food and drink in our practice of hospitality.

If I got to invite one of the Bible personalities to my table, then it would be Luke. More than any of the other Gospel writers, he seemed to understand the significance of mealtime. Based on his account, I know he'd bring to life the significance of food and community.

If you had an hour right now, I'd ask you to page through the Gospel of Luke and jot down any references to Jesus' meals. At first, you might consider it busy work, but after your notebook filled with one page, two, then three full pages, you'd begin to see a pattern and your jaw just might drop. Mine did.

Robert Karris says, "In Luke's Gospel Jesus is either going to a meal, at a meal, or coming from a meal."[1] How in all my years of reading Scripture had I not noticed this?

Take a guess: how many times do you think Luke mentioned Jesus' meals?

Food and gathering around the table are mentioned around fifty times in Luke's Gospel alone! Yes, *fifty* times. On nearly every page, he mentioned food.

Why do you think he wrote about it so often?

Jesus used the sharing of food throughout His ministry as an opportunity for nourishment on so many levels: to break down barriers, bring community together, radically cross economic boundaries, and even give opposing enemies the opportunity to sit together.

He knew a meal . . .

> . . . was never simply a time to ingest food and quench thirst; at meals
> people displayed kinship and friendship. Meals themselves—the foods
> served, the manner in which that was done and by whom—carried
> socially significant, coded communication. The more formal the meal,
> the more loaded with messages. The messages had to do with honor,
> social rank in the family and community, belonging and purity, or
> holiness. Social status and role were acted out in differentiated tasks
> and expectations around meals, and the maintenance of balance and
> harmony at meals was crucial to the sense of overall well-being. Among
> God's chosen people, meals became ways of experiencing and enjoying
> God's presence and provision.[2]

But one of the most fascinating insights came from how Christ's eating tied in so closely
with why He came to earth.

> There are three ways the New Testament completes the sentence, "The
> Son of Man came . . ." "The Son of Man came not to be served but to
> serve, and to give his life as a ransom for many" (Mark 10:45); "The Son
> of Man came to seek and to save the lost" (Luke 19:10); "The Son of
> Man has come eating and drinking . . ." (Luke 7:34). The first two are
> statements of purpose. Why did Jesus come? He came to serve, to give
> his life as a ransom, to seek and save the lost. The third is a statement of
> method. How did Jesus come? He came eating and drinking."[3]

Isn't that dynamic insight? How brilliant that Jesus' gospel strategy was often disguised as
a long, lingering meal that stretched out after sunset. He didn't spend time creating more
corporate planning strategy meetings or growing new church programs. He simply fed
and gathered at the table more. His message and His method were woven together in
such an authentic and natural way that we almost miss it.

The context behind many of Jesus' interactions with His followers was a simple meal. He
modeled its importance, and yet Luke seems to be the only one who highlighted this in
his writing. Maybe he didn't want us to miss out on Jesus' simple, revolutionary method.

How does this change your view of sharing meals with others?

Let's look at a few passages from Luke and fill in the blanks:

PASSAGE	SETTING/MEAL	GUESTS	OBSERVATIONS, REACTIONS
Luke 5:27-32	A banquet at Levi's home	Tax collectors and sinners	Matthew followed without hesitation. Jesus came for the sinners and the sick.
Luke 7:36-50			
Luke 9:10-17			
Luke 11:37-52			
Luke 24:28-32			
Luke 24:36-43			

Phew, that's pretty revealing, isn't it? How can we learn from this and apply it to our own lives? Jesus came "eating and drinking"—and it blew people's minds. Who would have thought the Savior of the world, the King of kings, the One who never hungers or thirsts would spend so much time eating and drinking?

When He sat down to eat, there was a lot more going on than just the savoring of fresh fish hot off the grill, a loaf of bread, and a drink. Doing life around the table was (and is) one of His favorite ways to enact world change—one of His most profound yet simple strategies for discipleship, evangelism, and the encouragement of the saints. So let's follow His lead.

When are you free for dinner?

DAY 2

The Five Senses

I'm writing this week's study curled up on my favorite sofa. A cozy, handmade blanket that I snagged at the thrift store lays across my lap and a faint breeze caresses my face. The wind rustles through the trees and the soft sound of birds sing in the background. I also happen to be out on my front porch sipping my coffee (splash of cream, thank you) and snacking on a muffin while I soak in my surroundings.

Each of my five senses are completely engaged, and the simple pleasures from being fully present in this moment aren't lost on me.

Won't you take a brief minute and do the same? I know you might be rushing to finish this, but put down your pen, take deep, cleansing breaths, look around, and engage your senses.

What do you see, hear, taste, smell, and touch?

Don't like what you see and smell? Light a candle, hang white lights, and study by the soft flicker. It does wonders for the soul.

Spending a few minutes each day to stimulate our senses can enable us to experience life and communicate love to ourselves and those around us in a new and fresh way. For the first time all weekend, I'm relaxing—kind of. My body aches from exhaustion, but my heart overflows from a place of abundance: soul-giving contentment that stems from belly laughs, inside jokes, and deep, challenging conversations around the table.

Two guests spontaneously whipped into town for the weekend, so I executed my two "must-dos" of hospitality. I implemented my tried and true, laser-focused cleaning method. (I affectionately call this my Ten-Minute Tornado Drill—I throw all the clutter into plastic boxes and put them in the attic.) And I stocked up on quick comfort foods. Nothing fancy. Frozen lasagna, ingredients for a simple soup, French bread, taco dip, and cookies.

For me, the kitchen is the heartbeat of our home. No matter how often I create gathering places in other areas, it's in the kitchen and around the table where the warmth of shared memories, laughter, and life create a recipe that spans generations. It's where the senses are engaged, a place where people are drawn to linger. The aroma of baked goods (frozen cookie dough works perfectly), the flickering candlelight during the evening meal (even when it's frozen pizza and boxed macaroni), the cut flowers donning the mason jars (dandelion weeds picked by our daughter), and the soft music floating in the background are only a precursor to the cornerstone of life found around the table. There's really nothing like it.

For our family and I bet yours too, the mundane and the magnificent intersect around the table, but it takes a continual heart prompting to realign and prioritize its importance.

> Read Acts 2:42-47. What do you notice the first church did together that we do not (usually) do in our churches today?

> Is there anything in these verses that we still do in our churches? If so, what? Why do you think those practices have endured?

1. THEY WERE DEVOTED TO MEETING TOGETHER.

In Acts 2, we witness how the believer's steadfast devotion to simple, everyday choices—God-honoring teaching, constant fellowship, prayer, and mealtime together—become the launching pad to their explosive revival in the church. It's been the plan all along to advance His kingdom through the table, but for me personally, the words "every day" or "daily" resonate most. I've shared before that I tend to get bogged down in the oh-so-daily moments of life with food and mealtime topping the list of unavoidable requirements. Often those become "have to" chores, yet over and over, I witness daily moments being the catalyst for divine appointments forged among our ordinary ones. The Lord delights in our everyday average. Isn't He so good and gracious like that? He doesn't require or expect anything fancy; we put that pressure on ourselves.

It's in our seemingly-common, day-by-day, hour-by-hour, mundane invitations that we are called to be faithful first. Nothing beats the life-giving abundance that comes from choosing to be deeply rooted right where He has us: around our everyday table—the place the Lord prepares in advance for me and my family, the place that He prepares for you, wherever that may be. When His table intersects with ours, it offers the only food and beverage that truly satisfies our deepest cravings: a table laden with glory and grace.

2. THEY ATE WITH JOYFUL HEARTS.

The second theme that resonates was that "they ate [received] their food with joyful and sincere hearts" (v. 46). The Greek expounds to offer exultation, specifically, "gladness" or "exceeding joy."[4]

I asked myself, *When we gather at the table, does it represent a time of exceeding joy? How often do I mumble and complain about the simple act of preparing or offering food rather than acknowledging with great thankfulness that it all came from Him?*

> Be honest. Does gathering at the table bring you joy? If not, what could you do differently to help curb your complaining?

It reminds me of Peter's exhortation:

> Offer hospitality to one another without grumbling.
> **1 PETER 4:9, NIV**

Grumbling in this day and age often means excuses: "I don't have extra money in my budget. It's too much work. I don't really like to cook." When I find myself with those immediate reactions I reframe my attitude toward the ultimate goal of proclaiming His glory.

Meals together are small acts with significant importance. They allow for holy moments to happen when we slow down and let them.

So how can we shift the atmosphere of our homes so that when we break bread together, we all experience the encouragement that Paul wrote about in Philemon?

> For I have great joy and encouragement from your love, because the hearts of the saints have been refreshed through you, brother.
> **PHILEMON 7**

One of the ways I show a tangible yet experiential love is by first engaging the five senses.

As small children, our five senses are drilled into us during our preschool years. However, as we reach adulthood, we often forget their importance. Senses welcome us, warn us, comfort us, nourish us, soothe us, and encourage us.

No matter our hesitations to hosting, whether it's the status of our house or time constraints from a busy schedule, I know we can all agree that there's such joy in creating a home where family and friends are comforted, where stresses of the day are washed away, and where guests yearn to pull up a seat and stay. Creating an environment that communicates love and breathes life to those in it is often simpler than we ever imagined.

Lay aside your worries about a perfect table, and embrace your five loaves and two fish. Remember, no house is too small that one more can't be invited. When I would host in my tiny apartment, I'd remind myself that small is the new big and cozy is the new grand.

> Close your eyes and try to remember a simple yet significant meal experience. What was the occasion? What made it special? How can you reproduce this in your own home? (OK, you can do this exercise with your eyes open, but right now I'm looking at three baskets of laundry that need to be folded, so it ruins the ambiance I'm trying to envision.)

There's something incredibly powerful about engaging our senses in such a way that special memories and traditions are intricately woven together around food, isn't there? Food holds memories and instantly engages the senses.

Our senses are a gift that allow us to become more acquainted with the majesty of God.

> In what ways can we can honor Him through our senses?

> Use a Bible concordance to find one Scripture that corresponds to each sense.

One of my favorite verses perfectly expresses my desire for table time.

Read Psalm 34:8.

I love this from *John Gill's Exposition of the Bible:*

> *He is essentially, infinitely, perfectly, immutably, and solely good in himself; and he is communicatively and diffusively good to others: he is the author of all good, but not of any evil, in a moral sense; this chiefly regards his special grace and goodness through Christ: all the divine Persons in the Godhead are good; the Father is good, he has good designs towards his people, has provided good things for them, made good promises to them, and bestows good gifts on them: the Son is good; the good Shepherd that has laid down his life for the sheep; he is the fountain of all grace and goodness to his churches, and to particular believers; he has wrought a good work for them, the work of redemption, and he speaks a good word on their behalf in the court of heaven: the Spirit is good; he works good things in the hearts of the sons of men, and shows good things unto them; and gracious souls, such as the psalmist here calls upon, are capable of tasting and discerning how good the Lord is in some measure.[5]*

Are we inviting others into a life that makes people want more of our good God? Do we model joy and celebration for all He's done in our lives?

In what ways are you doing this well, and in what ways could you do it better?

Because here's the thing: When you look in my fridge, my favorite foods all have an expiration date. They're temporal and don't last long, but what God offers—His goodness, His pleasures, His presence—never expires. What He offers should mark our homes, our families, our presence in such a profound way that anyone around us can't help but want what we have.

Read Revelation 19:6-9. This is the table we all want to gather around, the ultimate supper, "the marriage feast of the Lamb."

In verses 6-7, what are some of the actions shown here that we can bring to our own table?

When guests gather, may we celebrate and praise. May our homes reflect our love of life and our table testify to His goodness.

We're cultivating a lifestyle of table fellowship so that we'll be able to think back, not just on the meals eaten here, but on the life we've wrestled through and the stories lived out around our table. I want the table to be a place that reflects sacred moments and a love of nurturing life. Because when the mundane and the magnificent intersect around the table, a sense of identity is forged. It's where we shape our worldview, process our history, dissect our theology, debate our politics, and both confront and restore relationships. All are allowed to flourish at our table.

How can we afford to deprioritize this time-honored tradition that holds the utmost importance from days of old, one that's based around a fundamental pattern we see outlined in Scripture? Why do we consistently overlook one of the simplest pleasures—to linger, savor, and enjoy our time at the table?

Let's reclaim it, prioritize it, and model His method so that our message is so intertwined in our everyday choices, we begin to look and sound and smell more like Jesus.

DAY 3

Forks and Spoons

Sitting in front of me are pages and pages of additional notes that won't fit into this study. There's so much to unpack, and the further I explore the overarching theme of biblical hospitality, the more passionate I become.

As I wrote this section, I read a paragraph to my friend and told her I was feeling a little fiery. She pondered it a bit and responded, "You're passionate, but in some of the sentences, it feels like you're thumping your fist on the table. Leave those out." I get her reaction. I really do. When I mention hospitality, women would much prefer to expound on yesterday's calming encouragement to engage the senses. Soothing music, lit candles, and fresh herbs from the garden sprinkled around the natural tablescape with quick tips for getting dinner on the table are hospitality ideas we can rally around. While I'd love to stay all safe and comfortable reveling in the sweet ambiance we created yesterday, Jesus was anything but safe and predictable. In fact, when it came to the table, He was one of the radicals.

Since our kids were little, I've reiterated the theme, "We need to fight for our mealtime," so the idea of a food fight (ha) isn't new, but when I saw an article titled, "Hospitality Is War," I knew I wasn't the only one who decided to take up arms. God delivers many tools to defeat the enemy, and some are masquerading as forks and spoons, with a side of casseroles and community.

Suit up your armor. Hold on tight to your coffee cup. The table's going to get a lot dicier, but it'll be worth it.

> *God has a habit of waging war with strange weapons. He fought Egypt with frogs, gnats, and boils. He defeated the Midianite army with Gideon's clay pots and torches. Strangest of all, he defeated sin and death using a tree. So, it should be no surprise to us that Jesus calls us to take up forks and spoons to fight back Satan and his legions.*[6]

When I think through God's strange choices, it begins to make perfect sense as I connect the dots. Hospitality is worship. Worship is a weapon to defeat the devil; therefore, hospitality is war. We expand God's kingdom as we share the truth around the table, and the enemy certainly doesn't want that occurring. All those excuses, all the reasons we try and convince ourselves that opening the door is too much of a hassle, should be viewed as part of the battle. Those doubts are part of his strategy to close your door for good, because he knows the table is one of the best places to enact world change. As God's people, engage and go boldly on the offensive. Grab some food to share, and snatch Satan's captives away from him by inviting them to your home. Set the table, pick up your forks and spoons, and prepare for battle against Satan's schemes.

Let's look at some of the ways Jesus fought back at the table.

> Read the account in Matthew 9:9-13; Mark 2:13-17; and Luke 5:27-32.
> Compare and contrast the different versions of this same story. Note what is unique to each telling of the story.

MATTHEW	MARK	LUKE

For added background, Jesus had been in Capernaum and was loved by many there. He'd come from healing the paralytic where people were astounded. News had spread about Him and overwhelming numbers gathered to listen to Jesus. But one man didn't. His name was Levi (Matthew).

Depending on your Bible version, two differing names are used. To avoid any confusion, some scholars suggest that Levi was the man's given name, whereas Matthew (meaning "gift of God") was given once he became an apostle and also aided in concealing his former profession.

What do you know about the tax collectors or gatherers during this time?

As a tax collector for Herod, the most despised occupation by Jews, Levi would have been considered unclean. A traitor for cooperating with the hated Romans, tax collectors were banned from synagogues. Scholar J. Jeremias says,

> *Anyone engaging in such trades could never be a judge, and his inadmissibility as a witness put him on the same footing as a gentile slave . . . In other words he was deprived of civil and political rights to which every Israelite had claim . . . This makes us realize the enormity of Jesus' act in calling a publican to be one of his intimate disciples . . . and announcing the Good News to publicans and "sinners" by sitting down to eat with them.*[7]

Some Jewish historians even note that repentance for tax collectors was impossible, the ultimate sinners, unforgivable. Wow, that's a heavy burden to carry for your choice of profession.

What occupations, if any, hold a similar stigma today? What about decisions within a job?

I'm sure Levi had heard the buzz about Jesus as most everyone had. Did it compel Levi to find out about this Jesus for himself? Was he with the crowd listening to Jesus? Was he searching for Him at all?

While Levi missed Jesus' teaching, the Lord never missed out on him. He sought out a despised man, someone the scribes described as a lawbreaker or robber, but that didn't stop our Good Shepherd. He initiated, pursued, and went to seek and save the one lost sheep, even though crowds surrounded Him and clamored for attention. He desperately cared about calling one unto Himself.

Look again at Mark 2:14 and Luke 5:28. What difference do you notice between these two versions of the story?

Levi left everything behind. The significance of this choice is astronomical. Only in Luke's Gospel was Matthew's willingness to drop everything and follow Jesus in complete obedience emphasized. This had significant impact because of the severe ramifications. Once he left behind this profession, he could not go back. He was turning away from all that he knew, including power with Herod, prestige, and more notably, a lot of money. Tax collectors were rich.

Has there ever been a time when you've been asked to give up something? Maybe it was something small but significant to you, or maybe it was everything you knew and held dear. Explain.

If you are a Christ follower, you are also asked to give up everything to follow Him. What has that looked like in your life?

When people get a taste of Jesus, everything else pales in comparison. They'll jump at the chance to follow Him.

Look at Luke 5:29. What did Levi do next?

Luke's account tells of "a grand banquet," which implies how excited Levi was to introduce Jesus to his friends. He wanted to throw a party to make a big deal about Jesus. He wanted his colleagues to meet and know Jesus the way he did. He wanted his old life and new hope to collide.

Mark used "reclining" (Mark 2:15) to indicate there was no hurry. When you recline, you're relaxed; you're not rushing. Because of Levi's social status, the only people he could invite were other sinners. He didn't have a lot of friends who would have been approved of by the parents, so to speak.

Before we continue, it's important to understand how radically countercultural Jesus' table time activities were in His culture. Meals weren't just about food. They were inextricably linked to social values and ceremonial laws. The table was separated and the line firmly drawn, because all were not welcome to dine together. There was a clear-cut demarcation between insiders and outsiders in families, communities, and ethnic groups.

> Gentiles and strangers either were excluded or had to undergo special ritual cleansing in order to participate in even ordinary meals. There were strict limitations on food, its preparation and its consumption, distinguishing between the ritually clean and the unclean. Concern for holiness, which gave rise to the kosher (kashrut) laws of later Judaism, reflect the Jewish conviction that God is present at meals. To eat defiled food or to eat with an "unclean" person would be inappropriate and dishonoring to God.[8]

This means that Jews never ate what Gentiles ate. They would not be caught entering their homes, and in no way would they share a meal together. It's the ultimate "us versus them" mentality, so when Jesus dared to welcome all to this table, He transcended social boundaries no one dared cross and did away with this great cultural and spiritual divide. Where did He do this radical work? He implemented it at the table.

I wonder if Levi became anxious while reviewing his guest list. I wonder if he worried whether Jesus would show up, if he worried about all of his guests getting along. What grace he experienced when Jesus not only showed up but reclined at the table, taking His time to eat with Levi's friends!

What question did the Pharisees and scribes grumble in Luke 5:30?

There's no way we can imagine the radical, cultural implications that Jesus made by dining with sinners. When the Pharisees, the epitome of self-righteous legalism, complained about Jesus crossing this great social and religious divide, they were battle ready. Misguided, but ready to take Jesus to task. As the most revered holy men in society, the Pharisees would not willingly cross paths with unclean sinners.

When questioned, Jesus responded with one of His most defining statements, which included a template for our next dinner guest list.

Boiled down to the bare-bones, He shared the plan of salvation in Luke 5:31-32.

Put these verses in your own words. What does this mean for you today?

Who normally gathers at your table? How does this tie in with the Great Commission?

We can all probably recall some strained extended family gatherings, but I can't begin to imagine the terrible tension that filled the room that day. It was anything but cozy, tame, and comfortable: the clean and the unclean fighting for room at the same table. Finger pointing, judgment calls, the whole works. Not that we want to seek out this kind of relational tension, but one thing I know for certain: Our table, like Jesus' table, should be one that offers radical, even scandalous, grace. To all. To anyone.

That's the message I want to live, and that's the invitation I want to extend. The most profound gift of hospitality we can give is the assurance, "You are loved and welcome at my table exactly the way you are. You are worth showing up for. Every day. All the time."

It's the Jesus way. The risky, relentless, and scandalous way. The gift of grace given without expectation of anything in return. Pointing others to the only One who will truly satisfy them: the Bread of life. So pick up those forks and spoons with a little comfort food thrown in, and utilize the most effective weapons we have to fight back against the devil. I'll see you at the table.

HOSPITALITY INVITATION

In a typical week, how often do you gather around the table with family or friends?

I fully understand the double-edged tension, so there's no guilt shaming from me. We have to eat to live, yet our schedules resemble a thousand-piece puzzle, and therefore something has to give. But as I look at the importance Jesus placed on gathering, it's convicted me to reprioritize this.

When we add up the amount of time afforded us to dine together throughout our lives, the resulting sum comes as a shock. By the time we reach our fortieth birthdays, we will spend more than forty thousand meals in a food-related atmosphere. That's a tremendous opportunity dished up right before us, and yet, for most of us, a shift has occurred. I'm sure you've noticed it.

> *We eat one in every five meals in our car. One in four of us eat at least one fast-food meal every single day. US households spend roughly the same amount per week on fast food as on groceries. Sixty years ago, the average dinnertime was ninety minutes; today it is less than twelve minutes. . . . The majority of US families report eating a single meal together less than five days a week. And even then our "dinners together" are mostly in front of the TV. No wonder the average parent spends only 38.5 minutes per week in meaningful conversation with their children. We are losing the table.[9]*

As we lose the table, we lose a generation of lives intertwined for His glory, and this week I'm asking you to fight for time around the table. Some seasons of life make spending concentrated table time more difficult than others, and wow, do I understand that struggle. Casting a long-term legacy begins with one small step toward intentionality and then guarding the importance of that single step.

> Look at your schedule and begin by setting a reasonable goal. Find pockets of time that make eating together four times a week possible.

It doesn't have to be dinner. It can be as simple as ice cream floats after a long day or inviting your next-door neighbor for a Saturday pancake brunch. You can do this, and the stories your table will tell can't be matched.

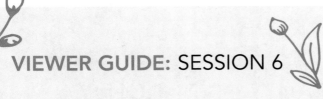

VIEWER GUIDE: SESSION 6

Watch the Session 6 video and discuss with your group the following questions:

1. Describe one of your favorite "at the table" or recipe memories.

2. Do you have a mealtime tradition? What has helped you to fight for meals together with your family or friends?

3. Why do you think gathering around the table helps break down boundaries?

4. Read Acts 2:46 together. Where have you seen holy moments of gratitude come from the "day by day" routines of life?

5. Jaquinn said, "We as a church, we get to model what it looks like for everyone else." Is the church doing a good job of welcoming others to our tables? Why or why not? How can your group model hospitality for the church?

Video sessions available for purchase at LifeWay.com/JustOpenTheDoor

WEEK 6:

THE UNCOMFORTABLE YES

I can't believe it's our last week together. To be welcomed at your table as I share a bit of my heart with you is such an honor.

We've covered a lot of ground, haven't we? We've shattered the image of needing perfect lives and perfect spaces and replaced it with something that brings kingdom relevance to our hearts and homes.

We've been challenged with how Jesus pursued and modeled a life of invitation. We've identified barriers and seen hospitality as worship and as war. Through it, my prayer is that you've been able to step back and say, "Yes, Lord. I'm willing to be Your one simple person. Here's my one door, my one sofa, my one table. Use them."

Isn't it humbling to realize we don't have to get our act all polished and perfected before He begins to use us for His glory? He has chosen us to champion His love wherever, whenever, and for whomever He puts along our path. We're not meant to do this alone.

I hope that message is sinking deep into your bones, because life is sweeter, kinder, and richer when we walk hand in hand with other women who fight for us, encourage us, cry with us, and laugh with us, and we in turn do the same for them. Through our small faithful steps of obedience, we're transformed more into His image. And full warning— we will need to rally all His power in us to view this week's topic as an invitation to act.

We're not finished yet. Normally people save the best for last; well in this study, I've saved the most challenging for last, but stick with me. This is going to require us to lean in with a full heart toward some uncomfortable hospitality. Maybe you're wondering, *Hasn't everything you've asked me to do included getting me out of my comfort zone?*

Maybe, but there's still so much more comfort zone stretching to go. For some of us, opening our doors hasn't truly cost us much. Maybe it's meant switching our calendar around a bit or taking the first step to realign priorities, but for the most part, it's been an exciting way to love and serve others. This week we're going to look at what giving an uncomfortable yes means to the heart of Jesus. A yes that gets our hands and hearts shaky. A yes that has us throwing little tantrums with ourselves because we do not want to do it.

What does it really look like when we put our comfort, security, and assurances aside and walk out hospitality and receive nothing in return? What if it means entering into some-one's pain and sitting with them amidst untold grief when we have no idea what to say? How about if it means being rejected or showing hospitality to those who have wronged us? Surely He can't mean that.

Do you see why I mentioned needing to access all of His power that is alive and active in us? He promises to be right there walking us to and through that door. He is stronger than any struggle, any fear, and any rejection you might face, and in turn, we will understand what it means to walk out all of God's truth. No longer will we pick and choose parts of His Word that fit into our lifestyles, but we will understand what it means to surrender all aspects of hospitality to Him.

Come on. This will be uncomfortable. You might even fight it a bit, but it will be so worth it in the long run.

P. S. You also will not want to miss the last video with my dear friend, Tammy. Her impact on my life points me to Jesus every day.

DAY 1

Hospitality Toward Difficult People

We gathered for prayer at the end of our Bible study, and my friend's request rang true for many: "I'm dreading that my extended family is coming for the holidays. It sounds horrible to admit, but I really don't want them at our house. We have broken relationships and someone always stirs the pot. I'm bitter, and it shows in my attitude when they're here. Please pray for me."

Difficult people. They're everywhere. In all aspects of our lives.

The aggressive in-law. The preschool mother who second guesses our parenting styles. The patronizing coworker. The ministry partner bent on sabotaging relationships. We could go on and on—a complaining spirit, a passive-aggressive friendship, a cocky neighbor. Where does it stop?

The reality is that we are sinful people in a broken world, acting out in ways that are anything but holy. Most days our lives intersect with those challenging people—and we don't know how to respond. In week 4, we discussed our worldview and asked, "How do we live our lives in view of what we know to be true?" Our family often dissects this question around our dinner table, and one conversation that repeats itself is the difference between our natural person and our spiritual person. Ask any of our kids and they'll be able to tell you.

Paul spent much of 1 Corinthians 2 comparing spiritual wisdom and earthly wisdom:

> The natural person does not accept the things of the Spirit of God, for they are folly to him, and he is not able to understand them because they are spiritually discerned. The spiritual person judges all things, but is himself to be judged by no one.
> **1 CORINTHIANS 2:14-15, ESV**

What is the natural person?

If you were explaining this to children in a Sunday School class, how might you differentiate between the natural and the spiritual person?

Even though we have received the fullness of God's love and we have His discernment to help us, often we choose to make decisions based on our natural person, which is our old person. We avoid rather than address. We ignore rather than invite. We let our feelings and desires rule us, rejecting the revelation, wisdom, and power that is made available to us through the Holy Spirit. We stir contention's pot ourselves.

And since I don't mince words with my kids, I won't with you. When we know the truth of His Word, have access to His power, but choose to reject His wisdom anyhow, that choice is wrong.

Ouch! It's much easier reminding my kids of that than myself. I didn't even want to write it out because people don't talk about sin much anymore. I've heard a time or two, "Who am I to say what sin is? Let's just love on everyone, because truth is relative." We're afraid to offend or judge. Plus, it's justifiable to leave someone whom everyone knows is unlovable, right? Wrong.

We are coming full circle here.

> I give you a new command: Love one another. Just as I have loved you, you are also to love one another. By this everyone will know that you are my disciples, if you love one another.
> **JOHN 13:34-35**

This sounds awfully familiar doesn't it?

We first heard this concept in Leviticus 19:18 and then Christ repeated it as the Greatest Commandment in Matthew 22:36-40. Used in this context, the Greek root for "new" is *kainos*, which "means 'new' in contrast to something old."[1]

How does John 13:34-35 denote a "new command"?

It is not so much that the commandment hasn't been given before as that it has a different quality about it, a quality of freshness that differentiates it from any other. To put it simply, this new commandment has "a new object and a new measure."[2] The object is now "one another." In the Old Testament the command was "love your neighbor as yourself" (Lev. 19:18). The Jews had watered down the Mosaic teaching so they could love whom they wanted and hate whom they wanted. But Christ changes the object from "neighbor" to "one another."[3]

This is an important differentiation, because now Jesus is speaking directly to believers. It's critical to note the context of this command: His final discourse. Jesus knew the time was coming for Him to leave, and I'm sure He felt a sense of urgency to impart His most important truths. He desperately wanted His disciples to live in unity and portray that to an unbelieving world.

With my son getting married in only a few short weeks, I've caught a teeny, tiny, micro-scopic glimpse of what Jesus may have been feeling: *Have I taught him all he should know? Is he ready for marriage? Does he understand that once the honeymoon is over unconditional love is a choice? That it cannot be based on her actions toward him?*

I remind my son that loving unconditionally involves surrendering your own needs for your spouse's; speaking and showing love even when he or she is undeserving, difficult, or hard to understand; living in peace with each other; and dealing with conflict immediately. Servanthood means—Ack! So much to share, so little time. My head swirls with the hard-fought wisdom I've learned through trial and error, but I can't get it all out fast enough. There's so much left undone. I can't imagine what Jesus felt.

> So we see in verse 34 that not only has the object of our love changed, but also the measure or dimension. Now He states, love others as _____.

Jesus laid down His life on behalf of undeserving sinners. This was new. Unheard of. His hospitality toward us was not an afterthought. Our Jesus knew what was coming, and He wasn't surprised. He spent His life anticipating that moment: the cross.

Difficult people denied Him, mocked Him, turned from Him, and Jesus chose this ending anyhow. Our rejection didn't keep Him from the cross.

Let's be super honest for a minute. Loving certain people is brutal, let alone sacrificing everything for them. It doesn't come naturally, so let's not try to pretend this isn't an issue on our minds. Often our desire is to give and receive love, but we want to give to and receive love from the pretty, the popular, and the lovable. That's easy love. A cleaned up, less messy version of authentically loving our neighbors that doesn't cost us much.

Yet we are called—no, commanded—to love the unlovable. Not just love them but love them well. But isn't that what we all are? Unlovable? And isn't that what Christ has done for us? Loved us well? I like how C. S. Lewis put it: "The rule for all of us is pretty simple. Do not waste time bothering whether you 'love' your neighbour; act as if you did."[4] We have a choice of whether or not we'll love others as we love ourselves and then that step further, as He loves us. A rekindled commitment to open-door living is one of the primary graces God gives us to shove our selfish, judgy, overly-critical resistance out of the way.

> Right now, think of one or two people in your life who are your spiritual sand-paper. (I like to think they help polish my rough edges to look more like Jesus rather than, "Wow, I really don't enjoy being around this person.") Keep them in mind as we continue.

> Reread John 13:35. How will others know we are His disciples?

> Have you ever noticed this about someone you know? What specific actions did they take that signaled to you they were followers of Jesus?

Jesus knew people would take notice. He desired His disciples' lives to look different from the rest of society, and this could only be achieved if they imitated Him. The same is now true for us. When we attempt to pursue peace with the most difficult people in our lives, both believers and non-believers, we take a completely countercultural approach to walking this road of welcome. A radical one, a sacrificial one—to love as He loves us.

He turned everything upside down when He commanded us to love our enemies, the difficult people, and to lay down our lives for each other as He did.

That's why when we love those who are difficult for us to love, it is undeniably of Him. And while we aren't usually put in situations where we literally have to give up our lives for another, we're called to surrender. Surrender our frustrations, our pride, our need to be right, our bitterness, our justifications and excuses for why we shouldn't have to because of all they've done to us. We're commanded to lay aside all that for others, for difficult people, for the ones you listed above. This is how the world will know we're His disciples.

Above all, put on love, which is the perfect bond of unity.
COLOSSIANS 3:14

Think through scenarios where you struggle to put on love. Make a plan to put on love (with the Holy Spirit's help) the next time you're in a hard-to-love situation. What will that look like for you?

This requires more than we can do on our own, and to get to that place is risky. It means mustering up a lot of bravery when we don't feel it and showing up for the everyday. It means advancing when we feel like retreating. Investing when we feel like withdrawing. Welcoming when worrying is so much easier. It's right in those moments when the wonder of the gospel is revealed in a new way—an opportunity to be image bearers of Christ, to be transformed more into His likeness so He gets the glory.

Now I'm going to ask you to take another step toward an uncomfortable yes. When you think back on what you've learned through this study, what is your role in hospitality when it comes to those difficult people?

Might God be asking you to initiate something new with a difficult person in your life? I know you'll have a list of reasons why it's too hard, but when loving costs us something, that is the true antidote to our own self-centeredness. Open-door living flushes out those tendencies to grasp for control. It requires surrender and sacrifice, but it roots us. It demands that we deny a lifestyle of lip service fueled by comfortable conversations. Open-door living is our invitation to act.

He is a God of patience and mercy, and He continually showers it on difficult people. Grace upon grace. As we've so abundantly received it, so must we pour it out on others. (By the way, what if we are someone else's difficult person and we may not even be aware of it? Raising my hand high on that one. I'd sure want grace, wouldn't you?)

The difficult people in our lives push us to a deeper level of dependence on God and prayer. We need the Holy Spirit to tutor us on loving in the hard places. We all have a choice. When it comes to loving others as Jesus loves me, I will continue to tell myself until I'm blue in the face, "I don't have to—I get to."

And that's exactly where I want to be. Join me!

DAY 2

The Ultimate Drop-In

We're on the homestretch, and everything in me wants to share with you every last scribbled note that I've studied. Don't worry, they'll never all fit. But wow, I never realized that the Lord would unpack so many themes that come from living out a life of invitation and welcome. He modeled every possible aspect of it and still continues to surprise me with more. Even so, I was stunned last Friday night when the doorbell rang and it was a friend I hadn't seen in two years who really wanted to talk.

I'd been snuggled in for a last final push of my writing. No make-up, three-day-old hair (don't care), sweatpants, sweatshirt, and since we're all ladies, the pinnacle of comfort after a long week—no bra. For dramatic effect, envision the state of my home. Cluttered counters from a week's neglect, a sink full of dirty dishes, boxes of clothes and books and miscellaneous junk that needed to be moved to our son's new apartment, and (cue the music—*dadadadum*) here I opened the door expecting to greet a UPS package left on our porch. My heart dropped to my stomach. Hopefully my dropped jaw wasn't as visible.

The dreaded drop-in. Another opportunity to lean into an uncomfortable yes, or more like a terrifying and paralyzing yes, even for the most flexible host. Can I see your hand if you've heard the doorbell ring, and your immediate reaction looked like something out of a grade school fire drill, "Stop, drop, and roll"?

We've all done it, although this time I wasn't even granted a "bra and broom text." Over time, I've grown in my habits of hospitality to where I can admit, "I'd love for you to pop in, but you need to send me a text first—enough time to sweep and get fully dressed." Can we not make that a thing?

> When your doorbell rings, what's your natural reaction? If you know it's a friend, are you comfortable inviting them in without notice? Why or why not?

An (in)courage reader commented. "My first instinct is to drop to the floor, crawl to the nearest window, peek out the blinds, and make no sudden movements. I've done it. Yes, I have." And, OK, she added, since we're all being honest here, "I've actually yelled to my kids 'Stay away from the windows!' so no one knows we're at home."

One of my favorite introverted friends confessed, "I can't do drop-ins no matter how much my heart wants to be OK with it because they cause me serious panic attacks." Instead, she's identified how God has wired her and has started a new tradition within her neighborhood group. Whenever she's ready to extend an invitation, she updates her Facebook status spontaneously with, "I'm ready for you. Drop in anytime between 10-2." I love that idea! She still welcomes others, but doesn't use her personality or her fear of the drop-in as an excuse.

So that's sort of the consensus on the drop-in. Maybe you register with some of those feelings and comments. But I recently started a knock-down, drag-out debate when I posed the following question on social media: "Is it ever acceptable for someone to invite herself over?" The responses ranged from "It's never OK. It's rude and selfish," to "Absolutely! Come on over, the more the merrier." This question doesn't have an easy answer. Truly the thought of an unplanned guest strips us to sheer vulnerability.

Here's the kicker, though: Jesus modeled the ultimate drop-in. He turned entertaining etiquette upside down when He invited Himself right on over to the house of Zacchaeus, the despised tax collector (publican).

> Read Luke 19:1-10. Jot down some key facts as you read.

> Last week we learned how tax collectors were viewed in Jesus' culture. Knowing that Zacchaeus was the chief boss of them all, from where do you think their complaints and murmurs stemmed (v. 7)?

> Why do you think Zacchaeus's decision in verse 8 is so noteworthy?

As the chief tax collector, Zacchaeus would have been skilled at the art of greed and corruption. Any additional taxes he collected above and beyond what the Roman Empire required added to his wealth. His prestige and privilege grew by plundering from the poor and common man without any thought to their plight.

By his promise to restore wealth and make restitution to those from whom he had robbed (four times—in line with a thief's punishment; see Ex. 22:1), he could have been wiped out financially since his coffers were filled through extortion. It wasn't necessary for him to repay anything, but his soul required more. His heart yearned for freedom from a debt that only Jesus could pay—salvation.

Since my first grade Sunday School, his beautiful redemption story has always been a critical theme (sing it with me, "Zacchaeus was a wee little man . . ."), but I found a hidden nugget that rocked my thinking on another aspect of open-door living.

If Jesus was the ultimate drop-in, how should that shift my heart in receiving that interruption?

Read Matthew 25:35-40. There's a correlation to be made there. What changes do you need to make in your heart and home to embrace drop-ins, the uncomfortable yeses, based on this passage?

Jesus knew the importance of inviting Himself over to Zacchaeus's house (right there in front of everyone, I might add). He let it be known that He wanted to hang with this tax collector, this wee little man hated by anyone with whom he rubbed shoulders. Jesus, though, deemed him worthy of time at the table, even worth the risk of appearing as an imposition.

What can we learn from this example about neighboring well—both as host and as guest? How can we practically apply this to our own lives?

Read 2 Kings 4: 8-10. The Shunammite woman gives us a starting place.

My brother, sister-in-love, and parents took their cues from this woman's hospitality. Driven by the idea of having a place of refuge for missionaries on furlough, my brother's family created "The Pineapple Place." It's a room above their garage specifically designated for any and all drop-ins. Ready on a moment's notice for someone needing a place to stay, they've had guests from more than twenty countries. My parents offer up their guest room, and they've housed more than fifty international students through the years. We are still only able to offer up a couch or our kids' beds as they share a room, but each option makes an impact.

We might need to chew on this one for a while, but in light of what Jesus did, can we still insist, "That's rude—it's always rude when someone invites themselves over," when this kind of radical hospitality turned an outcast host into a part of Jesus' story our kids still sing about?

So are you ready to receive interruptions as invitations to participate in something so radical, so life changing that your door becomes a beacon of joy that shares, "You're always welcome. Come as you are"? Or is there a sign nailed down that says, "Beware of dog"?

There's an invitation waiting to be received at every door, even those we'd never expect.

DAY 3

An Invitation for Everyone

And as I close this study where we've journeyed through a wealth of biblical texts that make hospitality both obedient and beautiful—or as I like to say, truly generation-changing—I want to finish by talking once again about hospitality and worship.

To remind ourselves that this gift of welcome we've all been given to radically offer up our lives as a willing sacrifice, to love others in a tangible way in response to God's command—it's worship. That doesn't mean there's not a cost to be counted. And, yes, sacrifice is definitely involved. But the leading motivation, the driving force, is a desire to worship God through the giving of ourselves—to know Him and to make Him known. And the joy that comes from obedience to Him makes it well worth it.

After all the times we open our doors scared, unworthy, unprepared, frazzled, or nervous, He proves that the risk is always worth the reward.

Let's revel in His reward, the promise of what's to come: the glorious fulfillment of God's greatest act of hospitality.

> Look up Revelation 7:9-17. Read these life-giving words of hope out loud.

> Describe what John, the author of Revelation, was seeing and hearing in this passage.

My whole heart yearns for the day when God demolishes all strongholds, when wrongs are righted, sicknesses cease, relationships are reconciled, and nations worship together in unity. But while we await this promise, we are to pursue this healing on earth as a way to bear witness to the return of Christ.

One of the ways we begin the healing process is by welcoming others who are different from us. The word *hospitable* stems from the Latin word *hospitalis,* or hospital.

> Do you see the connection between hospitality and a hospital? Explain.

As much as I long for that final feast with all the redeemed together, right now I'm called to throw my doors wide open so others get a glimpse of that reward, to help them experience a healing of the soul.

A while back, we gathered with a group of couples we hadn't seen in years due to a cross-country move. It filled my heart to pick up where we left off, to share victories and celebrate accomplishments, and lament over hardships. We'd walked through work difficulties, family failures, and even crisis of faith questions, yet freedom found its way to that table. It was a safe place. Hospitality is about so much more than welcoming spaces; it's creating spaces where we can each lay our wholehearted selves down and rest together in God's grace and goodness.

One of the gentleman looked around, visibly moved and full of joy, "This is just a glimpse of the goodness of heaven, isn't it?" We all agreed. This community of saints breaking bread together was a hint of His kingdom brought down to earth; yet the more I mulled over our night, I knew what was missing about his statement.

I personally hadn't risked anything to participate in that sweet community. It was a total gift I had received, but my hospitality wasn't a full representation of the kingdom. We all looked alike, thought alike, and believed similarly. One of our most challenging uncomfortable yeses will be choosing to be intentional about extending the boundaries to welcome more variety and diversity into our community circle. By enlarging it, we unearth the uniqueness that others bring to the conversation and most vividly reflect the true kingdom of God. Our triune God models unity and diversity. God the Father, the Son, and the Holy Spirit are one, and they each have different responsibilities and functions. This is the unity that God calls us to as well.

If you've already risked this and been rejected, well, you're in the best of company.

> Read Luke 14:15-24.

The basic message of this parable is a banquet of grace. The invitation is extended, the feast is prepared, and now we wait on who will come through the door.

Let's dive into this a bit more. The *CSB Study Bible* notes that "this story symbolizes being invited to the messianic banquet in the future kingdom of God."[5] Jesus told this story to religious leaders who assumed they would be in attendance for the banquet. The original invitation went out to people like them—religious leaders.

Look at the reception of the first group. What were each of their excuses? What might those excuses be today?

Why was the master so upset?

They rejected the invitation. Likewise, the religious leaders of His day rejected Jesus and His invitation to follow Him.

The host next extended his invitation to "the poor, maimed, blind, and lame" (v. 21). These are the people Jesus came to minister to, but there was still room at the table.

Who was invited to the feast next (v. 23)?

Those in "the highways and hedges" represent the Gentiles. For a Jewish man to invite Gentiles to a banquet in his home would have been scandalous.

Who ended up dining with the host?

How does this list compare to your regular invite list?

Now while beautiful in theory, and nice to aspire toward, this is where things start to get messy, right? There's a reason we like to stick with what's comfortable. There's a reason we prefer sharing the table with people who look, talk, work, and live the same way we do. We prefer the safety, the sameness, and the simple because it equals security.

But that's a total lie. Because following Jesus means taking risks. Following Jesus means asking and inviting. Following Jesus means hanging around with people who aren't our kind of people. Following Jesus means crossing boundaries and cultural divides—social, racial, political, and more—knowing this is the essence of the gospel.

What did Paul remind us of in Romans 15:7?

I like how the English Standard Version translates it:

> Therefore welcome one another as Christ has welcomed you,
> for the glory of God.
> **ROMANS 15:7, ESV**

Proximity matters, because only by developing real relationships with those who are vastly different from us can we begin to address the misperceptions that persist about Christian faith and the church, as well as listen to what others are really saying, even those with whom we disagree.

I know the truth of this, but let's be heart honest: the kinds of people Jesus hung around with on a regular basis aren't the people with whom I'd choose to hang.

Think back to all the passages we've studied. Who was on Jesus' invite list? Pharisees, fishermen, tax collectors. The deformed, the sick, the adulterers, the homeless, the refugees, the wanderers, the possessed, even the unclean. Risky individuals, all of them. Yet Jesus wasn't afraid of interacting with any of them—and neither should we be. We need to get up from our safe, anonymous distance behind our heated Facebook debates and our opinionated rants and actually live like Jesus lived.

Take a risk. Be real. Stir up the guest lists instead of stirring the pot. Extend radical grace that none of us deserve.

One last time, I'm going to get you a bit more uncomfortable. I want no miscommunication. This entire Bible study stems from Christ's scandalous love for us, but in our desire to love and welcome others, in no way should we compromise the truth of the gospel with something more palatable, not wanting to offend. We like to quote "Do not judge" (Matt. 7:1), but we forget the words printed just twelve verses later:

> Enter through the narrow gate. For the gate is wide and the road broad that leads to destruction, and there are many who go through it. How narrow is the gate and difficult the road that leads to life, and few find it.
> **MATTHEW 7:13-14**

Increasingly, those who call themselves believers are widening the gate on their own volition. Yet we noted in the parable of the large banquet that those who persistently refused the invitation to the great feast will forever be excluded from experiencing joy and life to the fullest.

John MacArthur once said in a sermon,

> [Jesus] exploded every time the false religious security of the Jews at every level, at the level of the Pharisees, the scribes and at the level of the people in the synagogues. Jesus always sought to shatter false religious hope. This is critical in all evangelism. This is being honest.[6]

And in our culture today, that's offensive. Yet as we approach this intersection of truth and grace, we must do better. We've been polarizing those around us, and we end up looking less like Christ than those who don't even know Him.

Where do you see examples of this?

Often we come to a diverse table with an agenda, rather than with humble hearts wanting to hear. Instead of asking thoughtful questions, we attack. Rather than listening, we implode. And when others don't agree with us, we no longer extend the invitation.

When we grow in our opportunities to love through differences, we proclaim God's goodness to those who observe it and set a table that surprises all with the freedom it represents.

So will we choose to be counted within the company of Jesus' dinner party—as one of the outcasts that He invited—or will we choose only to eat at the special table reserved for those who appear to have it all together? We have a choice. The pretty, polished, seemingly-perfect dinner guest is an awfully safe and comfortable companion, and that's who I've been drawn to more often than not. But I'm thinking that when we kick comfort to the curb, our table overflows to look a whole lot more like Jesus.

This whole concept of throwing open the invitation is risky. Another uncomfortable yes. Honestly, it makes me all sweaty and nervous when putting radical love into action, but I've begun to ask myself the hard questions:

Who is missing at my table? In my family room? On my invite list?

Am I willing to enlarge the boundaries of my heart to allow the core of gospel living to include anyone and everyone?

Does my table look like Jesus' table, set for all who are hungry and in need?

> Who is missing around your table—literally or metaphorically?

> Does your table look like Jesus' table? If so, how did it get there? If not, what can you do to make it look more like His table?

As I extend an invitation as Jesus did, as I pull up another chair, I can feel my heart opening up as well. It's risky, but the rewards are worth it.

I don't know if we'll ever truly understand hospitality as an act of worship until we open the door when we are completely empty, uncomfortable, and convinced we have nothing to offer. By making space to dig deep into both the joy and sorrow of others, we give ourselves margin to experience the most important things. Opening the door when we aren't ready defines *hospitality* in the deepest sense of the word. It's the exact place God wants us, and He guarantees He'll walk right to the door with us.

When we choose to bring our whole selves fully poured out, we bring our surrender and sacrifice to His altar. Once we've laid it all down, He picks it up, shifts it, and refines it. And when He hands it back, those blessings, the joy of open-door living, they're all worship.

Hospitality as worship.

All for You, Lord.

HOSPITALITY INVITATION

As we come to the end of our time together, we have the privilege to declare that our home and our hospitality offers us one of the greatest opportunities for kingdom change right at our very door.

God has no limit for all He wants to do in and through your invitations, so this week, dedicate your home to the Lord. Cast any fear or hesitations aside, pray boldly, and declare that you are ready and willing to widen your circle of influence for His glory. With full expectation, step forward in obedience, believing that your open doors will change your neighborhood, your workplace, and will radically impact those around you.

Invite your family to intentionally dedicate your home to the Lord and mark it as a place of welcome. When people walk through your door, you want them to have no doubt as to whom your allegiance points. Begin with a house blessing. As you walk each room, ask God to be fully present, specifying requests for that space and all the people who will enter your home.

FRONT DOOR—One of the most important assets to loving others is by starting at the very beginning: Just open the door. Invite the Holy Spirit to take control as soon as guests walk in and pray His loving-kindness would welcome them.

KITCHEN—Pray for the meals that will be prepared, the souls that will be fed, the conversations that will occur around the table. Pray that the drinks served will quench not just physical thirst but that guests will experience His "living water" (John 7:38).

LAUNDRY ROOM—Pray God would grant peace and stillness amidst chaos and that new life will be added to the daily rhythm of ordinary routines.

FAMILY ROOM—Pray the Spirit would surround those who gather here, that they will know Jesus is our firm foundation. Pray hope, peace, mercy, and forgiveness will fill this place.

BEDROOM—Pray for a place of unity, rest, and for respite during times of struggle. Pray protection over all who sleep here—spouses, siblings, roommates. For those who experience loneliness and desire connection, pray that God will meet those hidden longings in a way no one person can.

BATHROOM—When sickness hits, pray they will know God as the ultimate healer and that Jesus would surround them, hold them, and sustain them.

As you extend invitations, consider these aspects for your prayer time:

- We'd approach time together with grateful and sincere hearts (Phil. 1:3-11).

- We'd remember why we open the door in the first place (Col. 3:23).

- We'd see our invitations as a launching pad for kingdom purpose (Heb. 13:2).

- We'd discover joy in pleasing Him through our obedience (1 Sam. 15:22).

- We'd live with authenticity, so that our homes would be places of integrity (Titus 1:7-8; 2:11-12).

- We'd pray that His strength will manifest itself when we are weary (Phil. 4:13).

- We'd permeate the room with uplifting conversation, so that life-giving encouragement would flood the hearts of our guests (Rom. 15:1-2; 1 Thess. 5:11).

- We'd welcome others as teachable hosts. Ready to listen and glean wisdom from those who have gathered (Prov. 1:5).

- We'd gather with humble hearts of service looking to meet our guests' needs (Matt. 5:3; 1 Pet. 5:5).

Friend, thank you for journeying these last weeks with me. As I shared in the beginning, I want us to be able to look back in one year, five years, twenty-five years, and glimpse the legacy of hospitality we've offered. The doors we've opened, the chairs we've pulled up to ensure everyone has a seat, the tables extended so that anyone, from anywhere, knows they're welcome at our table—at His table.

I'm believing the Lord has already begun the multiplication process in your own life as you've declared, "Lord, I'm willing and available. Use me to point others to You."

Just open the door.

VIEWER GUIDE: SESSION 7

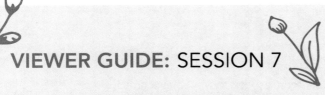

Watch the Session 7 video and discuss with your group the following questions:

1. Read John 13:34-35 together. Where have you seen Christians in our world doing a good job of following Jesus' command?

2. Do you have a "pivotal moment" in your life, like that of Jen's parents praying over their enemy, that changed the way you thought about loving others or showing hospitality?

3. Tell about an "uncomfortable yes" time in your life. How did you respond?

4. When have you needed your friends to help you choose an uncomfortable yes? Share the ways they loved you well during that time.

LEADER GUIDE

Just Open the Door is a video and discussion based Bible study. The weekly personal study, along with the teaching videos, will promote honest conversation as you study Scripture together. Conversation is essential to the experience, so some review and starter questions are provided. After your group has time to get settled, review the previous week's personal study, then join Jen and friends for that session's video. Use the provided discussion questions after to learn from one another.

TIPS ON LEADING THIS BIBLE STUDY

Pray. As you prepare to lead *Just Open the Door*, remember prayer is essential. Set aside time each week to pray for the women in your group. Listen to their needs and struggles so you can bring those requests before the Lord. Protect your time of prayer before each gathering. Encourage the women in your group to include prayer as part of their own daily spiritual discipline as well.

GUIDE. Accept women where they are but also set expectations that motivate commitment. Be consistent and trustworthy. Encourage women to follow through on the study, attend the group sessions, engage with the homework, and take up the Hospitality Invitations. Listen carefully, responsibly guide discussion, and keep confidences shared within the group. Be honest and vulnerable by sharing what God is teaching you through the study. Most women will follow your lead and be willing to share and participate when they see your transparency. Reach out to different ages, backgrounds, and stages of life for your group. This is sure to make your conversation and experience richer.

CONNECT. Stay engaged with the women throughout the study. Use social media, emails, or a quick note in the mail to connect with the group and share prayer needs throughout the week. Let them know when you are praying specifically for them. Root everything in Scripture and encourage them in their relationship with Jesus and the call to everyday hospitality.

CELEBRATE. At the end of the study, celebrate what God has done by having your group share what they've learned and how they've grown. Pray together about how God is asking them to open their doors as a result of this study of biblical hospitality.

TIPS ON ORGANIZING THIS BIBLE STUDY

TALK TO YOUR PASTOR OR ADMINISTRATOR. If you're leading this as part of a local church, ask for their input, prayers, and support.

SECURE YOUR LOCATION. Think about the number of women you can accommodate in the designated location. Reserve any tables, chairs, or media equipment needed for the videos and additional audio needs.

PROVIDE CHILDCARE. If you are targeting moms of young children, this is essential.

PROVIDE RESOURCES. Order a leader kit and the needed number of Bible study books. You might get a few extra for last minute sign-ups.

PLAN AND PREPARE. Become familiar with the Bible study resource and leader helps available. Preview the video session and prepare the outline you will follow to lead the group meeting based on the leader helps available. Go to LifeWay.com/Just OpenTheDoor to find free extra leader and promotional resources for your study.

EVALUATE. After each group session, ask: *What went well? What could be improved? Did you see women's lives transformed? Did your group grow closer to Christ and one another?*

NEXT STEPS. After the study concludes, follow up and challenge women to stay involved with others through another Bible study, church opportunity, or anything that will continue their spiritual growth and friendships. Provide several options of ministry opportunities the members can participate in individually or as a group to continue to apply biblical hospitality to their everyday lives.

SESSION 1

The following suggestions will supplement the discussion starter questions on the viewer guide pages. They are intended to assist you and stimulate discussion.

1. Ask "get to know you" questions: Where are you from? What do you do? Are you married? Do you have children?

2. What drew you to participating in a study about hospitality?

3. Describe what it means to feel welcomed.

4. Do you consider yourself to be hospitable? Why or why not?

5. What do you hope to gain from this study and our time spent together?

SESSION 2

For Sessions 2-7, consider beginning each week with an invitation to group members to share from their personal study by asking the first two questions below.

1. Would anyone be willing to share any experiences from your hospitality invitation this week?

2. Did anything in this week's personal study stand out to you anew, or maybe for the first time?

3. What preconceived notions and experiences shape your view of hospitality?

4. What theme did you sense in the biblical texts in the chart on page 18? How can we practically apply these passages to our lives today?

5. Share with the group the time you wrote about on page 21 when you experienced welcome.

6. Read Romans 12:10; Ephesians 4:1-2; and Colossians 3:12-13 as a group. What do these verses teach us about hospitality?

SESSION 3

1. Would anyone be willing to share any experiences from your hospitality invitation this week?

2. Read Psalm 139:1-17 as a group. Did any of the verses or phrases in this passage breathe life to you this week?

3. On page 41, which words or phrases did you circle that you tend to do more naturally? How can you begin to live more like the words and phrases in the left column?

4. How did the stories and verses in Luke 15 impact your understanding and practice of hospitality?

5. What do you immediately think of when you hear the word *worship?* Did your definition change this week? How so?

6. Make a list together of ways you can take hospitality on the go. Challenge each other to try out one idea this week.

SESSION 4

1. Would anyone be willing to share any experiences from your hospitality invitation this week?

2. Did anything in this week's personal study stand out to you anew, or maybe for the first time?

3. We studied several women from the Bible this week. What do their stories teach you about God's ministry model? Why do you think He chooses to work this way?

4. How have you seen God working in the midst of a difficult situation in your life?

5. Read Colossians 3:2 as a group. How can you cultivate a habit of focusing your mind's attention on God?

6. Have you ever had someone mentor you? Think outside the box. Who has poured into your life and taught you about God?

SESSION 5

1. Would anyone be willing to share any experiences from your hospitality invitation this week?

2. Did anything in this week's personal study stand out to you anew, or maybe for the first time?

3. Which do you identify with most—the doer, the doubter, or the I don't think so? Share why with the group.

4. What does your calendar say about your priorities? What would you like it to say?

5. Read Luke 16:10 and Colossians 3:17 as a group. Why do you think these verses can be used as a litmus test for the way we use our time?

6. Share with the group what you filled in the blank on page 102. "When He calls me, He will _____."

SESSION 6

1. Would anyone be willing to share any experiences from your hospitality invitation this week?

2. Did anything in this week's personal study stand out to you anew, or maybe for the first time?

3. Why do you think Luke wrote about food so often?

4. How does Jesus' example of using a simple meal for ministry purposes change the way you view sharing meals with others?

5. Read Acts 2:42-47 as a group. What did the church do then that we still do today? Why do you think those practices endured?

6. Who normally gathers around your table? Were you convicted this week to change that? Share some ways you plan to invite new people to your table.

SESSION 7

1. Would anyone be willing to share any experiences from your hospitality invitation this week?

2. Did anything in this week's personal study stand out to you anew, or maybe for the first time?

3. Read John 13:35 together. How will others know we are His disciples? How have you seen others live this out?

4. Discuss the connection between hospitality and a hospital.

5. Does your table look like Jesus' table? If so, how did it get there? If not, what can you do to make it look more like His table?

6. How has this study changed how you think about hospitality? What changes have you made (or do you plan to make) to just open the door?

ENDNOTES

Week 1

1. *Field of Dreams,* directed by Phil Alden Robinson (1989; Universal City, CA: Universal Pictures, 1998), DVD.
2. *The Sound of Music,* directed by Robert Wise (1965; Century City, CA: 20th Century Fox, 2000), DVD.
3. Walter A. Elwell, "Hospitality," *Evangelical Dictionary of Theology* (1997). As printed online at www.biblestudytools.com. Accessed 30 Jan. 2018.
4. John Piper, "Strategic Hospitality," DesiringGod.com, August 25, 1985. Available online at www.desiringgod.org.
5. Spiros Zodhiates, *The Complete Word Study Dictionary—New Testament* (Chattanooga, TN: AMG Publishers, 1992), 66.
6. James Strong, "G4355," *King James Strong's Bible II: Strong's Concordance* (TruthBeTold Ministry, Nook, 13 Oct. 2017).
7. "Philoxenia," *Vine's Expository Dictionary of New Testament Words.* Available online at blueletter-bible.org. Accessed 13 Dec. 2017.
8. Martha Stewart, *Entertaining* (New York: Clarkson Potter, 1982), 15.

Week 2

1. Frederick C. Mish, ed., "Do You Know the Origin of *omniscient?*", *Merriam-Webster's Collegiate Dictionary,* 11th ed. (Springfield, MA: Merriam-Webster, 2005).
2. Henry Burton, "Lost and Found," *The Expositor's Bible: The Gospel According to St. Luke* (London: Hodder and Stoughton, 1890), 318-319.
3. James Strong, "*poreuomai,*" *Strong's Greek Hebrew Dictionary,* G4198.
4. Ibid., "*bastazō,*" G941.
5. Ibid., "*baros,*" G922.

Week 4

1. Elisabeth Elliot, *Passion and Purity: Learning to Bring Your Love Life Under Christ's Control* (Grand Rapids: Baker, 2002), 163-164.

Week 5

1. Robert Karris, *Eating Your Way Through Luke's Gospel* (Collegeville, MN: Liturgical Press, 2006), 14.

2. Leland Ryken, James C. Wilhoit, Tremper Longman III, eds., "Meal," *Dictionary of Biblical Imagery* (Downers Grove: InterVarsity Press, 1998), 544.

3. Tim Chester, *A Meal with Jesus* (Wheaton, IL: Crossway, 2011), 12.

4. Ibid., *Strong's*, "agalliasis," G20.

5. "Psalm 34:8," *John Gill's Exposition of the Bible*. Available online at biblestudytools.com. Accessed 5 Jan. 2018.

6. Chad Ashby, "Hospitality Is War," 28 Feb. 2017. Available online at desiringgod.org. Accessed 5 Jan. 2018.

7. Joachim Jeremias, *Jerusalem in the Time of Jesus* (Philadelphia: Fortress Press, 1969), 311-312.

8. *Dictionary of Biblical Imagery,* Leland Ryken, James C. Wilhoit, Tremper Longman III, eds. (Downers Grove, IL: IVP Academic, 1998), 544.

9. Leonard Sweet, *From Tablet to Table: Where Community Is Found and Identity Is Formed* (Colorado Springs: NavPress, 2014), 9-10.

Week 6

1. William D. Mounce, *Mounce's Complete Expository Dictionary of Old and New Testament Words* (Grand Rapids: Zondervan, 2006), 472.

2. R. Kent Hughes, *John: That You May Believe. Preaching the Word* (Wheaton, Crossway, 1999), 331.

3. Adapted from Keith Krell, "3. Love Power (John 13:31–38)." Available online at https://bible.org. Accessed 7 Jan. 2018.

4. C.S. Lewis, *Mere Christianity* (New York: HarperCollins, 1980), 132.

5. "Luke 14:16-20," *CSB Study Bible* (Nashville: Holman Bible Publishers, 2017), 1636.

6. John MacArthur, Sermon: "An Invitation to God's Great Banquet," 9 Oct. 2005. Available online at www.gty.org. Accessed 7 Jan. 2018.

COME AS YOU ARE,
AND FIND YOURSELF AMONG FRIENDS

BE ENCOURAGED. Take a moment to breathe by beginning each day with a passage of Scripture and a story of everyday faith from this collection of 365 devotions written by women whose stories echo your own.

AVAILABLE WHEREVER BOOKS ARE SOLD.

(in)courage

He has called, equipped, and appointed you to do amazing things *right where you are.*

Look for those opportunities.
Seize those moments.

Just Open *the* Door

Because **one** invitation has the power to **change a generation.**

"How are you really doing?"

In today's busy world, we're wired to appear "fine," warding off authenticity and shielding ourselves from judgment. We hide behind the hum of busyness to escape intimate friendships with the women God has placed in our lives.

But we do want a seat at the table. We yearn for authentic relationships and the opportunity to be the opposite of "fine" with people who cheer for us. But comparison, envy, and entitlement often stop us from pulling out a chair at the table. Friendship can be hard, making new friends even harder, and maintaining genuine friendship the hardest of all.

In this 7-session, video-driven Bible study, Lisa-Jo Baker and friends from (in)courage explore our relationship with Jesus as the ultimate model for authentic friendship. Nothing shapes us like the impact of a friend—it's how Jesus radically and intimately connects with us. So instead of chasing perfection, overcome your fear of being known and find the courage to connect.

Bible Study Book 006103971 $12.99 | **Leader Kit** 005790530 $69.99

(in)courage
FIND YOURSELF AMONG FRIENDS